ADVANCE PRAISE FOR
Life and Leadership Lessons

"Nathaniel Noertker is a natural storyteller. *Life and Leadership Lessons* is full of heart, honesty, and hard-earned wisdom. It's the kind of book that makes you reflect on your own journey while cheering for his. I'm so proud of him for writing this—and I highly recommend it. A must-read for anyone navigating career growth while trying to stay grounded in values and family."

—Amishi Takalkar,
CEO and cofounder of Nailbiter Inc.

"*Life and Leadership Lessons* is a great book. As a person who just transitioned with my job to a new city, I found it to be absolutely encouraging. It allowed me to see that taking a chance was not a mistake. But you have to keep God first in your life. Take everything that you go through as a lesson. Everyone can get something out of this book."

—R. Robinson, vice president, Fifth Third Bank

"In *Life and Leadership Lessons*, Nathaniel Noertker shares an inspiring journey of taking control of his career amid personal and professional challenges. His chapter on the value of leadership coaching highlights its transformative power. This powerful narrative underscores how coaching can unlock potential and foster growth, offering valuable life lessons that aspiring and current leaders can embrace. Nathaniel's insights serve as a reminder of the importance of support and mindset in overcoming obstacles and achieving career success. This is a great book filled with practical and inspirational insights!"

—Valerie Plis, CEO, StrengthsBuilders LLC

"*Life and Leadership Lessons* inspires readers to trust in their abilities and place faith in God's plan. With heartfelt stories and practical insights, it guides readers through navigating career setbacks and overcoming personal struggles. This is a must-read for anyone seeking encouragement, direction, and the motivation to transform their own story."

—Eric Petree, pastor, Citygate Church

Life and Leadership Lessons

LIFE AND
Leadership
LESSONS

FROM *Rural America* TO
CORPORATE EXECUTIVE

NATHANIEL
NOERTKER

ISBN: 979-8-218-67492-2 (Print)
ISBN: 979-8-218-67493-9 (Ebook)

Cover and Interior Design: Nate Myers
Cover Imagery: Adobe Stock

CONTENTS

PREFACE

Life and Leadership Lessons: From Rural America to Corporate Executive is an autobiography of my life and the key lessons I've learned about leadership along the way. This is a book to help showcase key challenges we face, ways to overcome them, and how to utilize those experiences to make ourselves better leaders for others.

What type of scenario are you currently facing in your career? Are you in a leadership position with little experience and training, or potentially no training at all from your company? Are you struggling with trying to mentor someone on how to be a better communicator or presenter, or are you personally receiving feedback about needing to improve your own presentation skills? Do you want to enhance your career, but you're not sure where to start or the next steps to take? I talk about each of these topics throughout the book, utilizing moments from my own life and career where I've faced these challenges and more.

Growing up in rural Ohio had its limitations. I was limited not only by a lack of experience with other cultures and people, but also by what was provided within educational opportunities and knowing what was available beyond school. However, I tried not to allow these limitations to define me or keep me from achieving my goals.

I started my career in the grocery industry over thirty years ago as a bagger at the local grocery store, and I have worked my way up through the industry ever since. Over the last thirty years, I have pushed myself to learn from my mistakes, as well as others' mistakes, to grow my career and help develop my teams. Along the way, I've held roles of increasing responsibility within various aspects of the grocery industry.

I've worked inside stores with customers, in retailer corporate headquarter offices, at a brokerage firm, at major consumer packaged goods manufacturers' regional and corporate offices for some of the top brands globally, and in market research as a senior vice president in one of the fastest-growing market research firms in the world. Most of my career, across roles and companies, has been spent focused on the understanding of shopper behaviors in store and online to help brand teams and retailers bet-·ter meet the needs of their customers. Across those organizations and disciplines, I have led people for over twenty years from teams as small as four to over twenty. In each phase of my career, I have learned different tactics and approaches to become a better leader for my existing and future teams.

I've also learned over my career that what drives me is watching others I've managed, trained, and mentored go on to be successful in their own careers. I have had the pleasure of managing or mentoring multiple analysts and managers. One of the managers I worked with was fantastic at pulling together compelling information and building relationships with her customer contacts; however, she struggled internally with key leadership in our company. She was receiving feedback about not being able to take criticism or listen to others' opinions on the team. We worked on this together, resulting over time in positive feedback from internal leaders. This manager has since gone on in her career to be a very successful director.

I have worked with analysts who were so focused on the details that they missed the larger story of what was important, and others who were so nervous about presenting that they weren't able to showcase their knowledge and understanding of the data in a clear way (resulting in challenging feedback from senior leaders). Working on these key challenges allowed each of them to overcome critical feedback and develop their careers by showcasing the strengths and skills they brought to their organizations.

I have also had the privilege of working with many other younger team members over the years. I still connect with several of these previous team members on a regular basis to provide career guidance or just to catch up on their personal lives. Having the opportunity to connect with them, reminisce about our time working together, and hear how they are doing in their careers is so much fun for me. It is also an honor when they tell me about something we did during their training or mentoring that has had an impact on how they work today. They have all gone on to become team leaders, directors, and senior directors. Knowing that I've played a small role in helping them achieve their own goals is something I am very proud to have played a part in, and it has inspired me to put together this collection of lessons learned from my life.

Therefore, I hope this book helps you in your journey. I hope you find a situation or scenario that speaks to you and helps you determine the best path forward in your own leadership journey. Within this book, each chapter is set up to share a scenario from my life or career that will address one of the key questions mentioned earlier, and the lessons I've learned from each will provide you with insights and advice on how to resolve these issues in your own career. Additionally, I share some of the broader life lessons I've learned, and how my faith and my relationship with God have helped me in each step, often without my realizing it until much later.

Early Connections and Their Lasting Impacts

I grew up in southwestern Ohio, outside the small village of Newtonsville. When I was growing up, Newtonsville was a small town with just one four-way stop. I remember the Firemen's Festival with the parade that went through the village; grabbing candy being thrown, and riding the carnival-style rides in the middle of a field. The village grocery store on the corner, where you could grab some essentials or visit the deli counter for the freshly sliced cheese or the "fancy" bologna, was a frequent stop to grab a drink and a snack. Pap would often get the KB bologna, so anything with a national brand name would be the "fancy" kind. And I remember Mom stopping by the one gas station in town to get five dollars in gas to get us through to the next payday. At that time, five dollars would get you about half a tank.

Next to the grocery store was the one-room post office, and on the other corner of the four-way stop was the general store where you could find just about anything you needed; although what you needed was likely stored in an old coffee tin that would be placed on a random shelf that only the owner would be able to locate for you. Of course, behind the main counter of the general store was the long shelving rack of various guns available for purchase.

Today, the village has been officially dissolved, and the general store and corner grocery stand have been abandoned and are now falling apart. The gas station is long gone, and the main source of anything within the former village is the Dollar General store. What was once a thriving small village has turned into a run-down shell of its former self.

Our home, located just outside the village, was a ranch-style brick house with three bedrooms and one bathroom. It sat on just under an acre of land. Across the street was a corn field (or a soybean field, depending on the year), meticulously maintained by a local farmer. Best of all, about two miles up the road was Mamaw and Papaw's house. Papaw (Pap) was an over-the-road truck driver and was gone most of the time. Mamaw (Mam) didn't work outside the home when I was quite young, so summers were mainly spent with her while Mom and Dad worked to provide for us kids.

I am the youngest of three kids to parents who spent their careers working in the grocery store. Working as the managers of the meat department and deli department of the local grocery store provided for the family and allowed us the occasional road trips to various out-of-town locations. We had what we needed physically, and we had lots of family and friend connections throughout our time as kids to help us grow into the adults we are today.

As I went through school, I don't remember ever really having anything that stood out to me regarding what I wanted to be when I was older. I took the career placement tests in school, but the results weren't overly inspiring for me. They said I should be a counselor or social worker, or I should go into accounting. Of those, the latter was the most interesting to me, so I decided to focus my schooling on business and accountancy.

Looking back at my time in high school, I often wonder if the school counselor knew how much she had impacted my life. School was generally a challenge for me. It was not challenging because of the work or studies that needed to be done, but because of the bullying I had to endure each day. I was a heavy kid in high school, which resulted in a lot of challenging interactions with others, especially in gym class. My freshman and sophomore years were miserable. It wasn't the jocks who you would typically think of as the instigators of the bullying, but rather, a few who I now suspect may have had more challenging home lives. I hated being there, and other than spending time with a few close friends from the band, I tried to keep to myself.

Early in my sophomore year, the school guidance counselor approached me in the hall and told me she needed to speak with me. I typically didn't connect very often with the counselor, so I was curious what the conversation was going to entail. Once in her office, she mentioned a new program called postsecondary that would be starting the next year, which she wanted me to consider. The postsecondary program would be available to Ohio high school students with a certain GPA who wanted to get a start on college classes early, and she felt this could be a good option for me. She was absolutely correct! I could go to school, learn, and not have to worry about potentially being bullied on a regular basis. However, there would be challenges for me in taking this path.

Because this was a new program in the state, and because I attended a rural school district, the board of education in the district wasn't exactly supportive. I'm sure if the board had known that the counselor had approached me and informed me of the program, they would have likely reprimanded her. Why? Within the state, if a student decided to utilize the program, the school's funding would be shifted to the college to help cover the costs of tuition, books, and parking. Therefore, you can see the challenge the districts faced: help their students, lose their funding.

One way the board tried to discourage students from participating was by removing the college GPA weighting of the courses taken in the program. This meant that any course taken at the actual university would be weighted the same as a basic course at the high school level, and any AP course taken at the high school would be weighted higher than the course at the college level. Thus, my first learning opportunity for public speaking arrived.

I decided to fight the school board's decision. One of my classmates and I decided to go to the board meeting and object to the change in the class weighting policy. When the public comment portion opened, we both took the opportunity to speak. At sixteen years old, I was extremely nervous to try and convince a room full of older adults that our view was the right one. We had to showcase the reasons why, and the emotions behind our desire to attend college instead of high school in our junior year. We talked about the challenges of trying to truly learn in a public-school environment where teachers were being forced to focus their time on behavioral challenges in the classroom instead of instruction. We showcased our desire not to run away from the school we had grown up attending and where our friends were located, but to focus our efforts on true learning in an environment where students wanted to—and had paid to—be there. In the end, we asked not to be punished for our desire to enhance our learning opportunities.

Fortunately, our arguments were heard, and the board reversed their decision. Lesson learned. Put together your speaking points, back them up with facts and details, and provide your audience with a compelling argument. Also, utilize emotional connections to your key points to help your audience better relate to your point of view.

Thanks to the postsecondary program, I graduated with my high school diploma on May 31 and received my associate's degree on June 7. During my last two years of high school (which were also my first two years of college, thanks to the postsecondary program), I worked two jobs to save the money I'd need to attend college after graduating from high school. The two jobs I was blessed to work in were very different roles, each of which provided a great set of experiences for me.

First, I worked for a grocery store called Bigg's Hypermarket. This was an enormous grocery store focused on consistently low prices. While Bigg's doesn't exist today, its closest comparison store would be a Walmart Supercenter. In this job, I worked all the various aspects of the front end: register, service desk, layaway, training, and cash office management. The layaway department was a fun job in the store.

For those who may not be aware of what layaway is, it provides an opportunity around the holidays for shoppers to purchase gifts for their kids or loved ones without using a credit card. For example, the customer would go through the store and pick out their desired items. They would then bring those selections to the layaway department in the store. We would scan the items into the system, box and label them, and then we would store them in a marked location that was added to the computer for when the customer returned to pick them up. The shopper would make payments on their items throughout the season, with their final payment being due a week before Christmas. Working in an area where shoppers often struggled financially, the layaway department was well utilized. I remember my first Christmas season in the department. We had so many layaway orders that we had filled multiple storage rooms within the building (one room being multiple stories) and an additional nineteen semitrailers. Layaway was organized chaos, but it was a lot of fun for a detail-oriented person. There was something satisfying about being able to easily locate one shopper's order among all those products. Working in the stores, I learned about customer service, collaborating with challenging colleagues, and training others. I would work with the company for eight years, staying with them even after college.

My other job was with a large corporation that owned various other companies throughout the country. They owned companies in industries such as sportswear, insurance, financial services, logistics, and more, providing a high level of oversight. I was provided with the amazing opportunity of working with the company's assistant treasurer working on the company's SEC filings and various financial reporting. I only got the opportunity to work with this company by networking with their chief financial officer (CFO) during a leadership program I had been involved with in my senior year of high school. This was my first experience with a corporate role and what an actual accounting job could be, as I worked side by side with many of the company's accountants.

I continued to work for the company until a health issue eventually sidelined me for months.

The leadership program where I'd met the CFO was another instance where the high school counselor had impacted my life. While I was attending the University of Cincinnati as a member of the post-secondary program during my junior year of high school, my high school counselor reached out to ask me to stop by the school. I met her in her office as requested. She mentioned to me that there was a new leadership development program that would be starting in the county, and that she was recommending me for the program.

The program, Junior Lead Clermont, took two students (one male and one female) from each high school in the county, and put them together once a month for key experiences. In the program, we would get the opportunity to interact with government leaders and the judicial system, learn about our county's history, and meet with top business leaders in the area. Meeting with business leaders was what would lead me to connect with the CFO. In the session with the business leaders, I asked about what types of internship programs we should prioritize and when we should start to look for one. After the session, the CFO approached me and gave me his business card. He said he was impressed with my questions, and that he would be willing to help me with an internship when I was ready.

The postsecondary opportunity at the University of Cincinnati, and the guidance from my high school counselor, likely changed my life! The postsecondary program allowed me to start college classes during my junior year of high school, getting both college and high school credits for my classes, while the state paid for the college tuition. This helped me immensely as I'm not sure I would have had the money to cover a full four years of college. However, college wouldn't exactly go as planned.

Trust Your Gut

Have you ever had a time in your life when you've just felt like you knew what you needed to do, without any explanation for why? Or maybe someone in your life gave you guidance, or insisted you do something that you couldn't explain? Did you ignore that advice and later regret it? This chapter is focused on a time in my life when I relented and did what someone else wanted because of their "gut feeling" about the situation. In this circumstance, relenting and following their advice actually saved my life.

After a visit to Miami University in Oxford, Ohio, I decided this was the college I would attend to further my accounting studies. I made this decision because Miami University has a great business school. College was a challenging place for me socially. While being in the marching band should have provided many contacts and interactions with others, I did not have any social connections with anyone at the university. I have always been heavyset and not very popular. Therefore, making friends was a bit of a challenge, and I spent my time at college very much alone.

Coming into the university as a first-year student with the credits of a junior, I had a solo room in the freshman dorms. This resulted in me not knowing anyone in the dorm as I didn't have classes with them or really interacted with them at all. So, after class or band rehearsals, I would eat alone. I spent all my time alone. If I didn't go home on the weekends or chat with a professor about a class topic, I didn't speak to anyone for weeks at a time. It was a very lonely existence, and one that I do not remember fondly. I wish I had been bolder to meet other people, to build connections, and to help further my potential future—but I wasn't. I didn't learn the value of networking until much later in life!

During my second semester of junior year, I made the decision to contact an old friend from my time at the University of Cincinnati where I had taken my postsecondary courses. Out of the blue, I called her on a Wednesday. This continued each week on Wednesdays, until I had spent so much time on long-distance phone calls that my phone was getting shut off by the university. It took a good portion of my savings from working during the prior summer, but I got my phone switched back on so we could continue to chat. Our conversations continued to progress, and we eventually got married a couple of years later.

In my senior year at Miami University, now twenty years old, I noticed some lumps under the skin on my shins. I went to the dermatologist, and he decided to take a biopsy to ensure it wasn't anything serious. While I awaited the results, he prescribed prednisone and told me to take an aspirin a day to help curb the side effects. If you are in the medical field, you may have just gasped during that last sentence, and for good reason. This doctor's advice did not end well for me.

About a month after the appointment with the dermatologist, and after taking the medication as he'd prescribed, I was working to make some money to continue paying for my tuition and various expenses (like my phone bills). It was a Wednesday night, and I was working at the local Bigg's Hypermarket. I usually worked on the front end running a register or working at the customer service desk, but the deli department was short on people that night, so I was working in the deli for the evening.

This Bigg's location, where I worked during my college years, was the same store where several of my family members also worked. While I typically worked at the front of the store, my mom managed the deli, my sister worked in the bakery, my dad was in the meat department, my brother was in dairy, my brother-in-law was in produce, and my cousin worked in the pharmacy as a technician. We covered most of the store. Luckily, we all worked together well, and the store had a really good management team.

During this particular Wednesday night, I was helping my mom by covering a shift in the deli. Mom was also in the store that evening as the manager on duty. While she'd tried to switch with some of the other managers in the store, no one had been available. Therefore, she had been forced to also work in the store that evening.

While working, I was not feeling well. I felt so tired, and I noticed a general challenge to catch my breath. I could breathe, but my chest was tight, forcing me to stop every few minutes as I was getting quite winded doing very simple tasks. To get myself feeling a little better, I decided to wash dishes in the cooler and take a break from waiting on customers at the case. In the cooler, things continued to progress in a downward spiral.

While washing dishes, I continued to struggle to breathe, and I noticed I was sweating. Because I was inside the deli cooler, sweating should not have been an issue. I started to think I was coming down with the flu. I was about due for my fifteen-minute break, so I told my coworkers that I was headed upstairs to take a break and get something to drink. I was hoping that sitting down and hydrating would help me to feel better so I could finish my shift. I really just wanted to get through the night at work so I could go home and go to bed.

On my way to clock out for my break, I started to feel quite nauseous, so I went into the restroom and proceeded to get sick. I cleaned myself up, wiped my face with a damp, cold paper towel, and headed to the time clock to punch out. I swiped my badge to clock out, it beeped, and I hit the floor. I just couldn't stand up anymore. I was fully aware of my surroundings, so I knew I had not passed out, but I had no strength to stand or move. The store operator, who managed all incoming phone calls to the store, was behind her desk near the time clock. She was a petite woman, and I was a twenty-year-old obese young man. I heard the panic in her voice as she ran over to me. She singlehandedly dragged me over to a chair and helped me into it. She grabbed me something to drink, and I heard her, with a slightly elevated, panicked voice, page my mom over the store's speaker system for her to come to the break room.

I was starting to feel a bit better, but I was now quite embarrassed. My mom entered the break room with some haste, and got a rundown of the events from the operator before she came over to me to find out what was going on. I let her know I thought I was getting the flu, and that I needed to head home and get some rest. My mom refused. She was not comfortable with me heading home and insisted I needed to go to the hospital.

The idea of going to the hospital seemed silly to me. Why? I had the flu. There was no reason to go to the hospital when all they were going to do was check me out and send me home to rest. There was nothing they would be able to do for me that some rest and fluids wouldn't solve. We argued a bit about the next steps, but I ultimately relented and allowed her to take me to the ER.

Once we arrived at the ER, the check-in nurse reviewed my vitals. After checking my blood pressure, which was elevated, she had me stand so she could check my blood pressure again. When I stood for the vitals check, I got very dizzy and almost passed out. The nurse laughed and told me I had just won a night's stay in the hospital. She told me to go have a seat back in the waiting room and that they would bring me back shortly.

After some time passed in the waiting room, I was finally escorted back to a single room in the ER. The nurse who was helping me in the room was quite funny. She was cracking jokes with me and helping me settle in as she took more vitals and worked through her paperwork. My dad had now arrived and was in the room with me and my mom. The nurse proceeded to take a blood sample from me at the doctor's request, and she went to check on other patients.

As we awaited the results, the nurse stopped by several more times, always laughing and chatting with me whenever she was in the room. She was really helping me relax and enjoy the misery of being in the ER, but that was about to change.

The next time the nurse entered the room, the atmosphere shifted. She was straight-faced and wouldn't speak to me anymore. She was prepping things in the room with an odd determination but wasn't speaking. This was such a stark contrast from how she had been up to that point, and I started questioning her. For every question I asked, the only response I got was, "The doctor will be in shortly to speak with you." I asked another question, and I got, "The doctor will be in shortly to speak with you." I was starting to get a bit concerned, but I was mostly just confused. What had changed to shift her countenance to this degree? What had happened that had changed her entire demeanor?

The nurse finally left the room after having finished the various tasks she had set out to complete, and a few minutes later, the doctor entered. He started with a general question to me.

"How are you feeling?" he asked.

"I am exhausted! I feel like I have the flu, and I just want to go home and go to bed." I gave him this answer and told him I just needed to go home and sleep. What happened next will stay with me forever!

The doctor looked at me and said, "Well, I'm glad you didn't do that!" He then immediately turned to my parents and told them, "I'm not sure where it's from or why, but your son is bleeding internally. You need to start to make any necessary arrangements or phone calls to family, because I'm not certain he is going to make it through the night."

My mom left the room in a hurry, likely to avoid showcasing too much emotion in front of me. I knew she was just trying to keep from panicking me further, and she needed to get herself in order. The flurry of nurses and doctors began!

I was officially admitted. I had my stomach pumped, IVs started, and too many tests to remember.

Unfortunately, over the next several hours, my blood count kept dropping, and answers were nowhere to be found. No one seemed to be able to determine why or where I was bleeding from, or how to stop it. The tiredness continued, and severe pain started to set in.

The next evening, I was still in the hospital. Following a full day of tests and no answers, my blood count continued to drop. So I spent the next full night getting prepped for a colonoscopy. During this particularly fun time of preparation, my room phone rang. It was the dermatologist telling me that my results had come back negative and anything I was currently experiencing had nothing to do with him. What? I was sick and very medicated, but I knew this was odd. I would find out over a year later what this phone call had truly been about.

The test results came back, and the doctors had determined my bleeding was coming from my intestines. I was diagnosed with Meckel's diverticulitis. The recommended treatment at that time was to get my blood count back up and get me well enough to go home. It took a few days and four blood transfusions, but I was eventually released to go home and get some rest.

Over the next two months, I spent multiple days in and out of the hospital several different times, even undergoing emergency exploratory surgery where they went through every inch of my intestines to find the Meckel's issue. They never found anything! As a consolation, I suppose, the doctors removed my appendix, telling me it appeared to be inflamed.

This happened during my last semester of college, and I spent a good portion of that time hospitalized or recovering from having my stomach cut from above my navel to the top of my groin. Walking from building to building on campus and traversing the stairs within many buildings was a huge challenge. I was able to manage through the pain, but unfortunately, having many absences due to medical issues created consequences for my senior year of college.

While some of the professors in my courses worked closely with me to help me continue, two of them did not. I understood their perspective. I had been absent quite a bit due to hospitalizations, and this was not their issue. These two professors failed me, with one of them going as far as recommending that I drop out of school. This felt a bit unfair, honestly. I was a senior in my last semester, but with two classes I needed to retake, a challenging health situation, and a lack of funding to continue, I decided to step away from college and go full time into working after the semester ended.

About a year after my health incident, I was watching an evening news program when I learned why my health had taken such a drastic turn on that fateful night in the grocery store. The news program presented a story about the hundreds of people who die each year from the side effects of taking prednisone and aspirin together, as the combination causes internal bleeding. This was a major kick to the gut! The months of medical challenges and the near-death experience had all been because the dermatologist had been ill-informed about a medication issue. No wonder he'd called me while I had been in the hospital. He had been concerned about malpractice!

As I think back on this time in my life, I realize that if Mom hadn't been working that night in the store and insisted on a hospital visit, I wouldn't be here today. I would have died in my sleep that night. I would never have married, and my kids and grandson would not exist. Mom had been right to follow her gut that told her something was off.

I have learned over the years that each of us has those times when something feels off. We have those moments when we have no real explanation for the steps we are about to take, but they just feel right. Trust those moments when they happen to you! Those moments could literally change the course of your life!

LESSONS FROM
A CHALLENGING
MANAGER

Like many, you may have had a moment in your career when you had to work for a challenging manager. Maybe they were a micromanager, or they'd determined that managing with an iron fist was the best way to get results, or potentially they just didn't know how to be a leader. What did you learn about yourself during that time, and did it shape your leadership style? In this chapter, I will share about an extremely challenging manager I worked for very early in my career, and how that shaped who I wanted to be for others as I progressed in my leadership journey.

When I was out of school, after my struggles with my health and just two classes shy of a degree, I needed to focus on making money. So I went to work full time at the grocery store where I had worked to pay for my schooling. I spent the summer learning more about training and scheduling, and I ended up moving in the fall into an amazing role within the company's headquarters.

The new role required me to travel to all the various store locations the company owned, where I would train the store's personnel on new software and equipment the stores would need for Y2K. In this position, I further learned how to train others, problem-solved critical issues, and saw store operations more effectively from another viewpoint. Additionally, I gained experience with corporate travel and had the amazing opportunity to help grand-open multiple locations. This was one of the few roles I would ever regret leaving. So why did I transition to a new position within the company?

During one of the more challenging grand-opening events, I was helping troubleshoot and solve some critical issues occurring during the first week of store operations. What I didn't realize was that, at that same time, the company president was attending the grand opening of the store. I was informed later that he had requested I be placed back into a store to run a front end. So I left the role I loved and moved back into the stores as a part of the management team.

The store I ended up working in was a location that had been declining in sales for several years. From the store's peak performance to the current sales level was a little less than half the volume, but the front end was still structured with associate availability as though it were a higher-volume store. Additionally, the customer service scores were quite low. The challenge was to partner with the other front-end managers and tackle employee availability, scheduling, and overall customer service scores.

The front-end managers, the three of us, worked together quite well. In eight months, we reduced front-end payroll to the lowest percentage of sales within the company while also delivering the highest customer satisfaction scores across all stores! We were accomplishing all the goals we had set for ourselves when the store director decided that I should move to the deli department to do something similar. Shortly after moving to the deli department, the store director changed, and things went very badly for me. I learned many life lessons during this time.

The new store director was quite challenging. He ran a tight ship and had high expectations for each person on his team. I appreciated this expectation, and I was initially looking forward to him being on board. I felt like there was a lot I would be able to learn from him and his experience. However, one thing I learned was that this director had a reputation for selecting a "whipping person" in each store who would receive all his frustrations regardless of who the offending party to his mood was in the moment.

There was one incident where there was a challenge with the meat department in the store. It was either sales or payroll, I can't remember which one was the issue on that day. Unfortunately, my role in the store had become the "whipping person." Therefore, on this day, I was in the store director's office getting colorfully screamed at for the issues within the meat department. This was a memorable moment because I was in a situation where I didn't know how to respond. I was not aware of the issues, and I had no solution for how this other department should change what was being done. I was still quite young, and I had never experienced this type of management style. What was my role in this scenario? How did I, or could I, help solve the challenge? Do good leaders do this to motivate their team, or do they use this style of leadership to train younger managers on how to be more adept at the full operations of the store?

Several months later, a front-end manager position became available at a brand-new location that was not yet open. I reached out to the district supervisor I used to work with and expressed my interest in the role. She chatted with me about the store, and the conversation went very well. Unfortunately, this coincided with an incident that took place during our store's total store inventory.

During inventory, I took a break from counting to go to the restroom. As I exited the restroom, one of the front-end managers with whom I had previously partnered was covering the operator's desk while the operator was taking their lunch. This manager stopped me and asked me a question about the phone system. As I was answering her, the store director saw me talking at the desk. Instead of coming over to inquire into what was happening, he proceeded to scream at me from down the hall. While this was bad enough, the more challenging aspect was that the employee breakroom was between us. Therefore, every employee in the breakroom clearly heard what was happening in the hall. I was shocked by this and unsure of what to think about the situation. *How should I respond? What do I do?* Instead of confronting him right there, I turned and went upstairs to my desk to grab something I needed to continue inventory. I decided I was going to deal with the situation later when he would have had a chance to calm down, and when I would be able to share the details about the question I had been trying to help to answer.

Unfortunately, the store director went up the other set of stairs and cornered me at my desk. Now nose to nose with me, red in the face, and screaming, he let me have it. The other department managers who were upstairs at their desks all grabbed their things and left. Now, I was completely alone with the store director. Seeing his facial expressions, red facial color, and screaming, I truly felt like I was about to be punched at that moment. I didn't say a word. I let him use his various adjectives and colorful language, all while threatening my job. He knew there was another position open in the company that I was interested in, and he started to threaten me. He didn't like the idea of me leaving the store, and he suggested that he would fire me before he would allow me to transfer.

Once he finished screaming and threatening me, I didn't say a word. I gathered the items I needed from my desk, and I walked out of the building and straight to my car. I was done! I couldn't take any more of the verbal assaults. I got to my car and opened the door, and I was about to get in when my mind went to my family. I was married, and we were expecting our first child. A little girl. I knew at that moment that if I got into my car, I would never come back! So I shut the car door and told myself to get back to work. The responsibilities I had for my wife and daughter outweighed the challenges of dealing with this frustrating leader.

I soon departed from that store and moved to another location, leaving both the challenging store director and deli department behind. After that day and the many challenging experiences over several months with that leader, I vowed that my leadership style would look nothing like what I had been subjected to. I would do my best to treat people with respect, I would talk to them in the way I wanted to be spoken to, and I would challenge others when they created hostile environments. I would realize that each person should be held accountable for only what was in their control, and I would fully understand the situation before rushing to inaccurate judgments. Finally, I learned to always ask questions and be open to hearing the answers.

Now, thinking about a challenging manager you may have had in your career, what lessons can you take from those moments? How have they impacted you, and what will you do differently for your team? Each person we work for provides us with an opportunity to learn what we want to emulate and what we want to avoid. Take the time to look back on each leader you've worked for during your career, and map out the "emulate" and "avoid" characteristics you experienced. Which ones are you bringing to your team?

LEARNING GOD'S PULL
AND THE DECISIONS
THAT CHANGE OUR
LIVES

Over the course of your life, what key decisions have you made that have impacted the direction of your life or career? What factors have influenced your decisions in those moments? Were they driven by guidance you received from a friend or loved one? Were the decisions influenced by experience? Or was there an element of faith or belief in God that helped you determine your next steps?

My faith has played a large role in my life and the decisions I have made over time. While I often don't realize the full impact in the moment, looking back, I am always amazed at the guidance and direction God provides when I'm open to hearing His guidance. This chapter showcases one of those key moments in my life when I felt like God gave me clear direction about what I needed to do. Without this moment, I would not be where I am today. This one moment truly defined where I would be and what I would become in my career. Additionally, I'll share a deeply personal moment in my life when a leader basically told me that I wouldn't amount to anything in my career until I lost weight. The shock of that moment drove me, but it has also been the catalyst for a long-term distrust of others.

With our first child about to be born, I came to the realization that management in a grocery store was not the ideal scenario for our family. At this point, I had grand-opened another store location and I was working back on the front end. This resulted in a mix of work shifts each week, bouncing between first and second shifts; and on many occasions, a partial third shift to cover callouts within the team. Therefore, it was time to see what I could find for work with a more standardized schedule. This was when I learned about the brokerage world of the consumer packaged goods industry.

After working in the stores for many years, I knew we had vendors who came into the stores for various reasons. However, I didn't fully understand or appreciate what the vendors did while they were in the store, until I learned more about the brokerage industry.

The brokerage industry sits between the product manufacturer and the retailer. These companies often represent manufacturers across multiple disciplines, from selling new items, to performance analytics, to order management, and a variety of other areas. Brokers also have retail teams that help ensure items are on the shelf, or that displays are on the sales floor for customers to shop.

Through a former coworker and family friend, I learned that there was an opening at a national brokerage firm that could potentially fit my skill set. So I applied to the role.

After the interview process, I was offered a job as an administrative assistant within the health and beauty department focusing on retail reporting. It was a pay cut from my store manager position, but my wife and I both felt like this was a good move. We made peace with the decision, and we would make the finances work despite the reduction in pay.

What I later came to realize was that I would not have had the career I have today, nor would I have been able to provide for my family to the level I have been able to all these years, had I not taken that administrative assistant role. God was leading my steps, but I didn't fully realize this until later.

Once in the new job at the brokerage firm, I learned a completely new aspect of the grocery business I hadn't known existed. I worked diligently in my position to complete my work to the best of my ability, quickly learning that what was described as a full-time job during the interview process was nowhere near the amount of work the company had estimated. So I made the decision to ask for more work. This was also a key inflection point.

Asking the company for additional responsibilities within my current role allowed me to dive into another aspect of the grocery industry I had known little about: contracts and deductions. The brokerage company taught me how this process worked and how to be effective at writing these key documents, and they provided me with the insight that very few people are truly as detail-oriented as they should be. I got the opportunity to learn a great lesson on the importance of details from working on a very large manufacturer of kitchen gadgets.

I took responsibility for both contracts and deductions on a large kitchen gadget manufacturer. As I was getting into the details of the client, I realized that we were receiving multiple shipping holds on our orders because pricing was incorrect on the purchase order from the customer. So I requested updated price lists from my client to resolve the issues with the customer. This was where things got interesting. I found that not only did the customer have some incorrect pricing, but both my company and the manufacturer themselves had incorrect pricing listed for various items. I realized that the person working on the line before me had overridden price discrepancies to ensure orders would ship when needed, but she had not corrected the actual issue, which created multiple other challenges for both the customer and the manufacturer.

After reviewing all three pricing lists, I determined the correct price for each item and submitted paperwork to both the customer and the manufacturer to update pricing on all sides. Once processed, my orders started to flow with no issues. Shortly after I resolved the issues, I received an email that the customer's buyer wanted us to meet with him at their offices to discuss.

We arrived at the buyer's office and took our seats. Understandably, the buyer was quite upset with my client over the various issues that had been occurring. The buyer looked at my client and said, "You need to thank him [pointing to me], because without the work he has done in correcting all of these issues, you would be discontinued from our stores." I was shocked by the callout, but also proud of what I had been able to accomplish for my client. Key lesson learned: be in the details. My coworker who previously had responsibility for the client had not taken the time to understand or ensure that the key information had been correct, which had caused major challenges. If that person, and our client, had put in the effort to be in the details, the customer would not have had major issues with receiving products like they were experiencing. While you do not want to get stuck in the details, you should be familiar enough to fully understand and have confidence that the information you are relying on is accurate.

The situation with the kitchen gadget manufacturer and other key work responsibilities allowed me to shine in my first role at the brokerage firm. I received raises when the company said they were frozen, and I had strong client relationships by being willing to dive into the key details and nuances others would often overlook. It was a fun and educational role, but I desired more.

Another aspect of the brokerage industry I didn't know existed was a department called category management. The category management team was responsible for analyzing data for the manufacturers at the retailer level to determine what items should be on the shelves, what items should be on display, which promotions were truly effective, who was buying the products, how the shelves in the stores should be arranged, etc. I was fascinated! I had always loved puzzles, and category management was basically overseeing one giant puzzle.

My fondness for puzzles comes from my time as a kid. I remember being at my grandmother's house and helping her put together puzzles at the kitchen table. She loved them, and I think this rubbed off on me more than I initially realized. Therefore, I had a need to understand more. To the company's credit, they allowed me to spend time shadowing the category team. I saw firsthand what the category team did on a regular basis, and how they brought all the information to life for their key stakeholders. I was hooked!

After working in the administrative assistant role for almost two years, I decided that I wanted to try and get into category management. What I didn't realize was how many obstacles I would have to face in trying to do this. One, the company didn't want to set a precedent for moving administrative assistants into analyst roles. There was a traditional belief that administrative assistants didn't have the capability to work in more complex departments. Two, the company didn't want to take a chance on people who didn't have a four-year degree. And finally, they absolutely did not want someone calling on a manufacturer or retailer who looked like me. The latter challenge would be made very clear to me in the months ahead!

Once a position opened in the category management department for an analyst role, I applied. The interviews went very well, and I was already an employee of the company. I felt like I had a great shot of getting the role. Unfortunately, the hiring manager had no intention of allowing me to take the role in his department. Therefore, I was informed that I didn't get the role. There was no clear reason provided as to why I had not been offered the position, but I soon found out from his manager what the issue truly was with my candidacy for the role.

Within a week of being told that I did not get the position, the hiring manager's boss pulled me into an empty office to have a chat with me. Looking back, I appreciate the openness this senior leader had with me. Unfortunately, I did not have this appreciation at the time. I had to learn over the years to try and let some bitterness go from the conversation that day.

Behind a closed door in a spare office near my cubicle, our office's senior leader informed me that my background was strong and that I would be a good fit for the role, but if I continued to look the way I did, I would never get the job. He informed me that some people just couldn't bring themselves to "read the book" if the "cover wasn't appealing."

Did he just tell me what I think he did? Did he just tell me that my career would be determined by whether I could lose weight? I was shocked! The only thing I could bring myself to say was, "I understand." I felt gutted and betrayed. Why had I been working so hard in my roles at the company if the only thing that would determine my future was how I looked? The shock turned into anger, and the anger turned into bitterness. I would hold on to the latter for many years. However, the anger resulted in a weight loss journey I truly needed. I lost about 120 pounds over the course of the next twelve months. Sadly, but exciting too, I got promoted the same day I hit the mark of having lost 100 pounds.

During my weight loss journey, I was sitting at my desk at work, feeling miserable about the missed opportunity and the administrative work I was doing, when I felt a tug inside me to go back to school. I felt like something inside me was screaming, "Why are you sitting here? Why don't you call the college and see what it would take to graduate?" At that point in my life, I had been out of college for several years, and I wasn't sure what would be required to finalize my bachelor's degree. I was fearful about how many classes I would need to retake since it had been so long. So I reached out to the university and set up an appointment.

I was able to connect with a counselor at the university relatively quickly. She pulled up my record and informed me that the only thing I would need to do would be to retake and pass the two classes I had failed due to my medical issues. So my wife and I made the decision that it was time for me to go back to school. The challenge? We both worked full time, we had a young daughter, and we had another child on the way. My wife, to her credit, said that I should absolutely do it and that we would figure it out later. A few weeks later, we drove over an hour from our home to the campus to finalize my registration and get the necessary materials.

I will never forget the trip to campus with my pregnant wife and almost-two-year-old daughter. We entered the registrar's office and approached the desk. I informed the woman behind the desk what I needed, and she pulled up my information on her screen. She looked at the information and said, "I see here you are a nontraditional student." Now, while most of the sentence was stated at a normal volume, the "nontraditional" adjective was spoken at a whisper.

I couldn't help but laugh, and my wife and I still find a bunch of amusement in it to this day. A twenty-six-year-old guy, with his pregnant wife and soon-to-be two-year-old daughter, finalizing his college class registration? Yep! That sounded like a non-traditional student to me, and I wore that label with honor! Actually, I still do. I achieved a 4.0 GPA, and I worked hard for it! I maintained a full-time position at the brokerage firm, attended night classes over an hour from home two times a week, attended our doctor's appointments for our soon-to-be-born son, and helped raise our young daughter.

However, I look back on that time with a ton of fond memories. I only hope I was able to show my kids that, no matter what happens in life, you can do anything you put your mind to. I hope they can realize that, if they find themselves in a position or situation that they are not happy with, they have the power to change it.

Now, while the classes didn't teach me anything about my current career, they were what was needed to get my diploma. This piece of paper would open more doors for me in the coming years that would have otherwise been closed to me, and I wouldn't have that paper had I not been open to feeling God's pull. Understanding when He is leading, and being willing to step out on faith to undertake the challenges He lays out for us, are critical keys to growth! Be sensitive to His pull, and be open to doing what is required of you to make it happen. It will be worth it!

Finally, don't let others' opinions of you keep you from pursuing a dream! You can do anything you put your mind to, if you are willing to work to get it. There will always be people who will judge a book by its cover rather than taking the time to understand the real person, but those people aren't worth your time and talent. I still deal with these perceptions today, as I continue to struggle with my weight, but I remind myself regularly that I can do all things through Christ who strengthens me!

Awareness of the Gaps and Gaining Critical Experiences

As you progress in your career, how do you determine the skill gaps you need to close? Does this come from a good leader providing you with customized training to meet your needs, or do you need to change roles for the ability to achieve what is missing in your existing position? Another key area to focus on to ensure you have visibility for yourself is how you present and the effectiveness of your communication skills. Other than taking a communications course in school, what tactics do you use to learn these valuable skill sets?

This chapter will showcase where a great leader tailored her management style to help me grow, recommendations I use with my mentees about how to improve communication, and a moment in my career when a change in employer was needed to close critical skill gaps to enhance my long-term viability in the marketplace.

Having lost over 120 pounds in weight, I was permitted the opportunity to join the category management team with the brokerage firm. Now on the category team, I had an incredible boss named Lynn. Fortunately, Lynn was not the manager who had blocked my initial attempt to enter the department. While the other manager did have to see me every day, Lynn was incredibly supportive and challenged me in ways that stretched my skills. One of her leadership tactics that stuck with me throughout my career was how she interacted with me and helped me build the skill sets I needed in the future. Lynn was very good at understanding her team and tailoring her management style to meet each team member's needs. I like to believe that Lynn saw something in me that made her push my skills in a unique way.

Lynn lived over an hour from the office and often used her drive to think about the day and the various questions she had about each client's business needs. She was excellent at thinking through potential data we would need to build a solid strategy for our clients, and several times per week, she would call my desk line on her way home to leave me a voicemail with her thoughts. This became something I looked forward to each morning. I would come into the office each morning, anxious to see if my voicemail light was on, because I knew who the message would be from and what type of message it would be. Lynn's voicemails were generally a couple of minutes long, detailing her thoughts for the day. I took detailed notes and dived in.

Utilizing Lynn's notes, I ran various reports and researched her various hypotheses. It became a fun challenge each time she left me a voicemail. *Will I be able to answer her questions? Can I prove or disprove her various ideas?* I would spend the day researching and would often end up in her office later in the afternoon to walk her through the findings. We built a fun working relationship of learning the business while sharpening my analytics skills at the same time.

One of the other parts of the category department's job was presenting to retailers, and not only showcasing the findings of our various research topics but also helping the retailer to determine the next steps for their category. My role in this process was to arm Lynn with the data that she would present with our client to the retailer's buyer. I had a strong desire to be involved with the presentations, but our company's senior leadership was skeptical of my ability. Having never seen me present, the message was shared with me that I needed to join a presentation group or take classes from Dale Carnegie outside of work to help me get better with this skill set.

To Lynn's credit, she was confused by this feedback as much as I was, since she had also never had the opportunity to see me officially present anything. While she shared the feedback with me so that I would be aware of the perceptions from our leadership team, she was determined to help me showcase what I could do. Lynn started taking me to retailer meetings and allowed me to help answer questions about the data, and she eventually provided me with the opportunity to present a slide or two of data directly to the retailer.

The first time Lynn gave me the opportunity to present to the retailer, the presentation went very well, and the retailer was quite engaged with me during the discussion. After I presented my portion and the conversation moved to another meeting attendee, Lynn leaned over and whispered, "Dale Carnegie." I must have kept a straight face in the meeting, which was a challenge because I found her comment to be quite amusing. Afterward, Lynn provided me with good feedback on the meeting and reiterated her feeling that I did not need to pursue official presentation training as had been recommended by our senior leadership team.

I enjoyed my time on Lynn's team and learned quite a bit while in the role. Some key lessons for leadership I took away from this time in my career were ensuring that I supported my team members and provided them with the opportunities to learn through doing, and ensuring that I pushed to control the narratives about my team to the leadership above me. Unfortunately, as my time progressed on Lynn's team, I realized I had a gap in my learning plan that was likely to go unfilled within my current role and company.

While I was given opportunities to engage with the retailer's buyers during larger meetings, I did not get the chance to fully own the relationship while working with the broker. Showcasing that I could own the relationship and be successful at driving change at the retailer level was a critical component to my desired career progression. Therefore, I needed to look elsewhere to obtain this key skill set. Unfortunately, I made a mistake in my next role selection.

Instead of completely leaving my role at the brokerage firm and going to an unrelated organization, I made the decision to continue working on the same business line but working directly for the manufacturer instead of the broker. While this did have a substantial positive impact on my ability to provide for my family, the working conditions for this manufacturer were more challenging than I had anticipated.

The great boss I had at the broker was still a partner for me but was no longer my direct manager. I was instead placed with a manager who did not have the skill set to help in guiding me further with my analytics development, and who was quite an extreme micromanager.

While my new manager was also in a remote, work-from-home role, the requirements laid out for me were to work from the broker's office Monday through Friday. There was a nearby office for my new employer, but I was not permitted to work from that office due to intercompany politics. The nearby office was part of a different division within the company. Additionally, around fifteen to thirty minutes before the end of my workday each day, my desk phone would ring. If I was in the restroom or was getting water from the breakroom during this time of the day and I did not answer my desk phone, one of the broker's employees who sat near me would receive the phone call. My cell phone did not receive these calls each day, only my physical desk line. These calls had nothing to do with my work or a question my manager had, or the quality of my output; they were only to ensure that I was working in the office for the full amount of my workday. This was a challenge.

Additionally, I realized that the goal of filling a gap in my experience would not be able to be fulfilled in this role at the company as I remained on the sidelines while the brokerage owned the critical customer relationship. I would need to separate myself from the existing responsibilities and structure I had become comfortable with and place myself in a completely different environment to grow more effectively.

However, one skill set I had the ability to polish during this time of challenge came from outside of the work environment. While dealing with the new challenging situation I found myself in at work, outside the office, I decided to get involved in local government by running for office. I'm not quite sure why I made the decision that this was an area I should dive into, but it ended up being an excellent way for me to strengthen my ability to present to various people. Engaging with political competitors about a wide range of topics, either in front of journalists or at a town hall event, required me to quickly develop methods for dealing with nerves and learning body language cues from my audience about how well my message was, or wasn't, landing.

One of the town hall events during the campaign was televised, and a coworker at the time saw the debate on TV with his spouse. The next day at work, he pulled me aside to share with me some extremely valuable feedback. The coworker mentioned that both him and his spouse appreciated my views and stances on the key topics, but they couldn't understand why I had made a specific facial expression at the end of some of my statements. I was perplexed by this, being unaware that I had been displaying any facial cues during the event. The coworker then made the face back to me, and it was quite eye-opening. I realized that any time I was unsure or lacked confidence with a statement that I was making, I had a tell. This would become very valuable to me going forward, in knowing that I either needed to be better at being confident during my presentations, or I needed to be more conscious of the facial cues I was allowing myself to relay to others.

Another moment during the campaign that helped to shape me was an interview with the local newspaper. The newspaper invited all the candidates running for the elected office to come in for a small debate forum in front of the journalists writing the article. This was the forum the paper would use to determine who they were going to endorse for the upcoming election. Sitting in the room with several other candidates, who were all older and more experienced, was quite daunting. I was by far the youngest candidate in the room. *How am I going to cut through? Will I be able to stand out and not be dismissed for my age compared to the other candidates? Is my lack of experience in public office going to be a challenge?*

The forum at the newspaper office turned out to be a fun moment for me. While I was nervous at first, I decided to ensure that my voice would be heard. I made sure to call out others when I disagreed with their stances on the issues, while trying to do so without being rude or demeaning, and I made sure to give credit to the incumbents for key wins when appropriate. This worked well. While the paper did not go on to endorse any of the candidates who were not incumbents, I was the only newcomer to get mentioned by the article writers. They stated that, while they didn't feel I was quite experienced enough to gain their endorsement, they felt I had a promising future and could be a strong candidate in upcoming elections if I took the time to get more involved with the township government. So this was exactly what I was going to do.

Following the election, I continued to attend the township's public meetings. After one of these meetings, one of the incumbents approached me and asked me to join the board of zoning appeals. I agreed. I looked at this as an opportunity to continue sharpening my skills while learning a new aspect of how our local government worked. For the incumbents, I think this was a way for them to get me out of the way and keep me busy as the board of zoning appeals was mostly where all the angry people in the township went when they were frustrated by changes going on in the broader community. Over the next five years of serving on the board of zoning appeals, I had my fair share of articles written about me in the local paper, along with many angry, profanity-laden rants thrown my way while doing the job required of me. However, I would not have changed this time in my life at all. I ended up learning so much, not only about government, but also about myself, that the time invested ended up being very valuable to me.

Having spent over a year in a challenging situation of working for a manufacturer while based inside my former employer's offices, I needed to make another change. Through some mutual contacts, I was offered an opportunity at a new organization to showcase my abilities while working toward filling the gap of account ownership I knew I needed. It was a great opportunity, and one that would provide many excellent growth experiences.

When I started with the new organization, the local team was experiencing quite a bit of transitions. There were some medical leaves currently underway, some retirements getting ready to start, and attrition from the team in general. This provided a challenging environment for training and consistency across the team. However, it was an organization where I learned a great deal about account ownership.

While working in this new company, I had the opportunity to own account relationships for analytics, not only within my category but also within various divisions of my main customer. This resulted in traveling to other portions of the country to work with contacts I had never met or engaged with previously, offering an opportunity to build new relationships and networks. I really enjoyed being in this role! I quickly gained traction with key customer contacts, gaining full responsibility for critical components of the category growth strategy. The expanded influence was not only at the corporate level, but also within some of the larger divisions requiring me to travel to several locations across the US. Within this expanded role, I learned the power of getting a corporate buyer into a store. Having the time with the buyer to walk the store's shelf conditions and discuss key insights from data analytics was extremely powerful and fun.

In one instance, I traveled to one of the West Coast divisions and met with the local buyer. I was sharing insights from some data analytics of the shelves and how the buyer could enhance category performance with some basic shelf changes. We were partially through the conversation when she jumped out of her seat, walked to her office door, and asked her assistant to cancel the remaining meetings on her calendar. The buyer then looked at me and a coworker from the local market and said, "Want to go run stores? I want to look at the shelf in person while we continue talking through the data." For the rest of the afternoon, we drove to different stores, talking about how the buyer could improve sales. This was by far the best meeting I had been in at that point in my career. I had made the right decision to move into this role at this organization. However, things would shift within the organization and at home.

While the transition to a new role or company can be a challenging one, it can also be very beneficial to your career by offering you brand-new experiences and opportunities to increase your knowledge base that you may not have been otherwise afforded. Therefore, make sure you take the time in your current role to think about the learning plan you need to grow into your next two roles. Once you have your learning plan of key experiences, you need to ask yourself whether your current position will be able to provide those training needs. If not, you may need to consider beginning the search for a new position.

My overall experience running for office was impactful for me and my career. It was so impactful that local government is something I now advise mentees to consider when they want examples of good versus bad presentation and communication skills. Going to a local government meeting to see how the officials handle themselves and communicate with the audience offers powerful lessons for younger workers who are just starting their careers. My advice is to go to a local government meeting. This could be a zoning meeting, a school board meeting, or a council meeting in your area. See how the board members' or local politicians' presentations or communication skills make you feel as an audience member. Additionally, monitor the other attendees at the meeting, and see how they respond. What do you like? What do you dislike? Are other attendees getting upset, or are they in agreement? Are their responses due to content, or how the content is being delivered to them? A skilled speaker can deliver challenging news in an effective way and can defuse the tension in the room in many circumstances. Use these learnings to decide how you are going to change what you do with your communication at work. The best part? This training is completely free and can be a valuable learning experience.

Putting Family First:
Course Correction
Needed

How is your current work-life balance? Are you able to spend the time with your significant other, your kids, or other key family members that is needed for them and you? Where is your focus? These are some challenging questions I was forced to ask myself in the early years of my career. While I was winning over key contacts at my customer and having success in my work, my wife and kids were suffering as a result. This chapter focuses on a time in my career when I had to make some challenging decisions not for myself and my career, but also for my family.

I continued in my role at the company, learning key components of the organization and managing a relationship directly with a key customer. Unfortunately, resources at the organization continued to be strained and caused many challenges with my work-life balance.

Now over a year into the role, the attrition continued, resulting in very few human resources on the team. When I had started at the company, there were four people within the analytics department and several sales team members. I was now the only team member left in analytics, and my key salesperson was on medical leave.

The director of the team was a great leader, despite what the resourcing challenges suggested. He was personable, willing to dive in where needed, and highly adept at maneuvering corporate politics within the company. He was open to listening to any challenges and attempted to cover the medical leave of the salesperson with whom I had been working closely for my main category. Unfortunately, he was now as stretched as I was, and he was struggling to keep up. The director's key challenge was truly understanding the extent of the issues the team was facing, while trying to maintain his responsibilities and those of some of his missing direct reports.

Being the only remaining analytics team member, all the team's work fell on me until replacements could be sourced. This resulted in very long working days. Most days, I would arrive at the office by 7:00 a.m. and leave around 5:00 p.m. I left at this time each day so that I could go home, have dinner with my kids, and be there to help get them into bed. However, between dinner and bed, and after the kids went to bed, I needed to power up my laptop and work on key projects until some time between 11:00 p.m. or midnight each night. This happened daily. I never missed a deadline for any of the work needed, but it came at a high cost.

Along with the long hours during the week, my weekends were spent working around family events, and each vacation ended up being canceled due to work needs. Rightfully so, this started to cause issues at home. My wife was stretched because of my lack of presence, and the kids, while young, were consistently disappointed with cancellations and my lack of availability for them.

The critical moment came when I once again needed to cancel an upcoming planned vacation to cover the many needs at work. There was a new person on the analytics team who had been brought in from another team, but they did not know our customers' processes or systems. Therefore, they needed to be fully trained and could not cover my upcoming outage. Sitting in the office that day, I made a call to my wife and let her know we would need to cancel our vacation again. This did not sit well, and I knew we were getting into a tough situation as a family. I needed to make a change.

As if on cue, a contact of mine called me to see if I would be interested in helping a company develop their analytics team from the ground up. This other company was currently utilizing a broker but wanted to go direct with the customer and have the responsibility for the account in-house. My contact felt I had the skill sets and knowledge needed to be successful with their organization. This would be a great opportunity, and one that I could not pass, especially with my current work situation. So I made the decision that I would take a chance and go to an interview.

I had an initial interview with the direct manager of the role, and that went very well, but I could tell she was a bit inexperienced in her role. If I took the job, I would likely need to train my new boss in the key aspects of working with our key customer contacts. Knowing this, if I got the chance for a second interview, I would make the hard decision that I would have to be very straightforward in what I was looking for in a new role.

The second interview came, and the people in the leadership team above my first interviewer were very experienced. I appreciated their openness and experience, so I ensured that they understood where my focus needed to be within my next role. I told them that, while I would work diligently to ensure the work was done and that I was not opposed to working extra hours or days when business was critical, my goal was to have a work-life balance and prioritize my family at that time. I left the interview having a fun conversation, but with the realistic expectation that my directness may have cost me the role, and that was OK. I knew my priorities at that point in my life, and I was intent on focusing on them. To my surprise, I received a very strong offer from the company shortly after the interview.

With the strong offer received and the agreement on what the workload would be, I made the decision to depart from my company. Understandably, the director at my current employer did not take this well. He was facing another headcount loss with a current team that was severely understaffed and not equipped to fully manage the daily needs of the business. The part that hurt me during my departure was the lack of understanding of how much I had sacrificed for the team and how much I had done to make sure nothing fell short of our customers' expectations. The director made a comment to the team that I was departing because I wanted to make sure I had a nine-to-five job, and he insinuated that I was unwilling to work to do what needed to be done for the team. I remained bitter about that exit for a short time afterward, but I eventually ran into that director about a year later at the customer's office and had a great interaction with him.

About a year or so after leaving, the director who had been upset with my departure saw me in the lobby of our mutual customer's building. Standing there with my current coworkers, he called out my name and asked me to come over to him and the group he was standing with in the lobby. I was not sure what this was going to entail, but once I approached the group, he introduced me to the others who were standing with him. The coworkers he had with him were a group of very senior leaders from my old company: his boss, their boss, etc. He began to tell these senior leaders and his bosses that my departure had been his fault, and that I had been a great worker. He told them about how he hadn't truly realized what I had been doing for him and the company until I'd left, and that he wanted to personally thank me for what I had done while employed there. I was taken off guard with his statements. I was both impressed and moved by his honesty and willingness to admit a gap he'd had while being my leader, and the respect I already had for him expanded. I've never seen this director again, but I would love to be able to thank him for the valuable insight he gave me that day!

This powerful leader taught me a great lesson! Not only did I need to ensure that I knew what my team members were truly doing for my team, but I needed to own my mistakes as a leader and publicly acknowledge their true contributions. Additionally, making a sacrifice of a job or moment in your career for your family is sometimes needed, and that sacrifice may not actually be one at all. In this instance, the sacrifice of the role I left was far more beneficial to me in my career than I had realized.

Finally, ensure that you understand where your focus is and how that is impacting those around you. Your time in life is short, and your impact on your kids or family is greater than the impact you will have on a job!

LEARNING TO GROW UP
AS A PARENT

D o you currently live in the same area where
you were raised? Do you think about relocating to a different part of the country or world,
but struggle with what impact that will have on your
family? My wife and I often had similar thoughts.
We lived within thirty minutes of where each of us
were born and raised, and we were in the process of
raising our kids with the help of many immediate
family members nearby. Would a relocation be too
challenging for us or our kids? Could we be successful in managing life in a different area of the country?
Many people do it every day, but could we? In this
chapter, I will share our relocation story and what we
learned about ourselves in the process.

I spent the next couple of years building out the analytics team within my new company. As a team, we had a lot of success in building our capabilities but also engaged with our key customers. We went from being outsiders with our buyers to becoming trusted partners in a relatively short amount of time. How did we accomplish this task? Fact-based selling and relationship building.

I will never forget my first meeting with one of the toughest buyers I had ever worked with at this point in my career. Gary was a meat department guy who had worked his way up in the organization and was now overseeing the retailer's natural department merchandizing team.

I spent days, even weeks, preparing for my first meeting with Gary. I had analyzed the shopper behavior of the natural buyer in the retailer's stores within our category, and I knew I had strong data to showcase. While the data linked to our overarching story as a company, as it should have, it was based on facts that were coming directly from the buyer's own data. I felt very confident that we had a compelling deck with key actions that could be taken to improve the overall category's performance.

The first meeting arrived, and we went to the retailer's corporate offices to meet with Gary. He came out to greet us and took us to a conference room to review the information. I had printed copies of the deck for each person, hole-punched and bound of course, and I passed them out to the room and took my seat.

My boss got us started but quickly turned the meeting over to me so we could review the key data. Gary listened, somewhat, and I could tell he was growing frustrated. As I made my way through the deck, Gary flipped quickly on to the next page while we were still discussing the prior page. He also made sure to catch my eyes and wave his hands at me with a signal for me to speed up. Additionally, I saw him shaking his head, and I heard him providing random comments to ensure I knew he was irritated. About halfway through my presentation of our information, Gary stopped me. As I paused, he looked straight at me and said, "I would tell you that you are full of shit, but it's my own data." Gary then proceeded to toss the deck down the long conference table. As the deck went sliding past me on the long wooden table, I looked at my boss to my left and said, "I guess we are done."

At this moment, I knew what I would have to do while working with Gary. I would need to continue to stay focused on fact-based selling. I would need to ensure that everything my company did was focused on the needs of both the category and the retailer. I would have to make sure that anything we offered as a recommendation was backed by data and was completely unbiased, even if it was something he didn't want to hear. This would be the best approach to ensure Gary knew that what I was bringing to him could be trusted, even if it was challenging to review.

Fast-forward from that first meeting with Gary to just over two years later, and I was sitting at my desk in our company's local office when my phone rang. It was Gary. He asked me to come downtown to his office because he needed to see me. So I packed up my stuff and headed straight down. I walked to his desk, and he had me sit down. I wasn't sure what I was going to hear, and I was bracing for the worst. As it turned out, Gary wanted my help to complete something he knew I was quite able to do but that would require a lot of trust in me. This was personally a defining moment in my career! Putting in the effort of approaching each meeting with an intentional goal of working with him to build trust had paid off and would change how I worked with my own leadership across each role in my career going forward.

While I don't believe I ever told Gary this during our time working together, I always had a strong personal connection to him. As a child growing up with a dad, Garry, who worked in the meat department at the grocery store for his entire career, I felt as if in some way I understood him. I guess, in some way, I tried to seek his approval like a son would from his father. Getting that approval in the end made all the effort worth it. The last meeting with Gary at his desk ended up being the last time I had a chance to meet with him in an official capacity, as a short time later, my company offered me a role in the corporate office in Colorado. Gary even ended up coming to my going-away dinner my team held for me. Actually, he was the only person from the customer's team to join, making his attendance much more special to me. Thank you, Gary, for everything you've taught me!

The new role in Colorado was a great opportunity for my career, but it was a challenging situation to move my family over 1,200 miles away from everyone they had ever known. Neither my wife nor I had ever lived more than forty-five minutes away from our families, and with two young kids, this was going to be a big adjustment. We would have to grow up as parents, and as adults.

When relocating to Colorado, our kids were going into third grade and kindergarten. My wife and I, having always been very close to our families, were both concerned about our ability to truly be on our own. However, we made the decision to go ahead with the move. We sold our home in Ohio and relocated to Erie, Colorado, just outside of both Boulder and Denver.

We loved the area! From our front porch we could sit and look at the snowcapped mountains of the Rockies. Across the street from our neighborhood there was an amazing recreational center where the kids could swim and play, and both downtown Boulder and Denver were a relatively short drive away. We ended up having great neighbors on both sides of our home, and we were able to start connecting with others in the neighborhood and at a church we started attending.

The kids made quick friends in the neighborhood and at school, and as a family we set aside Friday evenings to go into Boulder and spend some time at the Pearl Street Mall. There, we would grab dinner and then take the kids to the local toy shop to browse the unique items available. Additionally, we made the time to travel around to different areas of Colorado to show the kids the beautiful state we now called home, including spending time in Rocky Mountain National Park and Estes Park, taking the kids skiing at Eldora, and visiting Colorado Springs, among other activities.

While all the transitions didn't go as planned, we learned that we could do it. We learned that we could make it somewhere outside of Ohio on our own.

Unfortunately, our Colorado adventures soon came to an end as I received unexpected news from work.

If you have an opportunity to relocate but are concerned about your ability to be a good parent or spouse, I recommend doing it. For us, although there were challenges that came with relocating so far away from where we grew up, I would not change that time in our lives as a family. We each grew and learned things about ourselves. We spent so much time together as a family, prioritizing seeing and doing new things. And without other family members close by, we grew closer as a family unit. I don't recall another time when our kids were growing up when we spent more time with them individually than we did during our time in Colorado.

So what life lesson did my wife and I learn? Separation from extended family, whether short- or long-term, is not always a bad thing.

HUMILIATED TO BLESSED

What are those moments in your career that you try to hide? Are there any situations or decisions you've made that you are embarrassed about? Is it truly something you should hide or be embarrassed by, or did the outcome set you up for something else that was better than what you had? In this chapter, I'll share about a time in my life when I was humbled, maybe even humiliated, by the way things had turned out in my life. I was humiliated by decisions I made. While I had to come to terms with the decisions I made in the moment, those events led me and my family to a much better place. Additionally, I will showcase the power of networking and how building a solid set of contacts in your industry can have a major impact on your career and personal life.

When we moved to Colorado, we moved for the long haul. We moved with the intention of staying and raising our kids there. We built a house, we planted ourselves in a church, and we started building local connections outside of work. What I didn't realize was that my company, with new leadership, was now in the process of restructuring the organization. Unfortunately, my role no longer existed in the new structure, and I found myself without a job. The spring of 2011 was one of the most challenging times in my life, and it contains my absolute largest regret as a father!

After having built a home ten months earlier, I found myself in the midst of a layoff process in an area of the country that had limited roles in the consumer packaged goods industry. At the same time, our sister-in-law passed away from extremely invasive breast cancer. Prior to relocating to Colorado, Jen had watched the kids almost every day. She'd had a big personality and heart, and she had been an amazing person and aunt. The kids had been very close to her, and her passing was very challenging for them. This is still something neither of them wants to spend too much time discussing, almost fifteen years later.

Upon returning to Colorado from the funeral, we started packing up our ten-month-old house so that we could place it on the market. I knew finding a job within the state of Colorado within my industry would be an incredibly challenging task. With my work experience and knowledge that a Cincinnati-based role would be much easier to obtain, we made the difficult decision to move back to Ohio.

The job search did not take long, and we started the process of building a new house back in Ohio. I was blessed to secure a job that paid more money than the role I had been laid off from, but the job required me to relocate prior to the end of the school year. Therefore, my wife and kids stayed in Colorado while I went back to Ohio to get started. For me, this was my largest failure as a father! While my intentions were to do what I thought was best for my kids and allow them to finish the remaining month left in the school year before moving them, it did not turn out to be the correct decision.

With a need to be back in Ohio to start my new position on Monday, I headed out for my drive to Ohio from Colorado, leaving my family behind. During this last month of the school year, I missed important events because of my job. I was absent from my son's kindergarten graduation, something I only got to see in pictures. I placed my family in an environment that was unstable: there was no husband or father around when there was a challenge, they had a house that was being prepared for a move across the country, and they were dealing with a close personal loss. My five-year-old son felt the largest impact of this, and for that I will never forgive myself.

To make matters worse, the new job back in Ohio was terrible. While this was likely exacerbated by my personal situation, I knew within two weeks that the company's culture and environment were not for me. However, I was brand-new and had a family over 1,200 miles away who were depending on me to provide for them. I couldn't leave the position, and I realized I would need to make the best of it. If I stuck it out for a year, I could allow us to settle back in Ohio, and then I could find a new job when things were not so hectic personally. I could make it work.

A little over a month after starting the new job, I made the flight back to Colorado to bring my family to Ohio. We had movers pack our things into some pods that were then sent to storage until the new house could be completed, and we all piled into the car and began our 1,200-mile drive. Once in Ohio, we made the decision to stay with my in-laws until our new house could be completed, which would be in about three months after our return.

Shortly after retrieving my family from Colorado and officially moving back to Ohio, a friend called me on my cell phone. He was a recruiter who specialized in the consumer packaged goods industry, and he was looking for someone to fill a role in the Cincinnati area that matched my background. This contact was someone who had helped place me previously in a great role and had helped run an organization where I had been previously employed, so I knew I could trust him. We had a very long conversation about my current situation, the newness of the job I was in, and the challenges I was facing. He convinced me to have a conversation with this other company. Despite my hesitation about potentially leaving my new employer so quickly, I made the decision to go ahead and meet with the other organization.

I was now approximately two months into my new job when I met with the other company's local contact. Surprisingly, this local contact was also someone with whom I had worked several years prior at another organization. Therefore, this new company's local contact knew me well and recommended that I interview within the corporate office the following week on the East Coast.

So, the following week, I flew to the East Coast and met with multiple people from the company. All the interviews seemed to go well, and the role appeared to be a good fit. However, the interviewers all knew that I had only been in my current position for a very short time. When questioned about my willingness to leave my current position, I was very transparent about the challenges I was facing at the organization. I was also transparent about my concern with leaving my current position so quickly. In each of the in-person interviews, the company's representatives were very understanding and thanked me for my openness, but I really didn't think this was going to go anywhere given the questions I was receiving about my current role. So I headed back to the airport to go home, with the hope that I may hear from the company within the next week or two. This was not the timeline that ended up occurring.

During my drive back to the airport, my friend, the recruiter, called me to chat about the trip and see how I felt about the process. I gave him the update, and we agreed to connect again in a few days once he had some feedback from the company. I ended the call on my cell and enjoyed the remaining drive to the airport.

After arriving at the airport, I made my way through security and headed to the gate to wait for my plane to depart. While I was sitting in the gate area, my phone rang, and it was the recruiter. I thought maybe he had forgotten to ask me something, so I answered the phone, ready to provide any additional details he may need. Surprisingly, he wasn't calling to ask me anything but rather to inform me that he had heard back from the company, and they were moving forward with an offer. Really? I was shocked by this call. I hadn't even boarded the plane yet. What he said next surprised me even more. He told me the new company wanted to know what it would take to get me to accept the job.

Stunned, I had no idea what to say to this request. I had been hoping something would work out to improve my working conditions, but I'd had no expectations that this trip would result in any ability to change my current situation. I also had major concerns about having to turn in a notice so quickly to my current company, and the potential impact this would have on my ability to close on our new home that was in the process of being built. But they wanted an answer, and they wanted it quickly.

So, consulting with my friend and recruiter, I asked for more than I thought the new company would be willing to give. I didn't want to completely sabotage the potential opportunity, but I needed it to be worth it! I needed to know this was what my next step was truly meant to be, given the challenges that would lay ahead in making this change. The recruiter took my feedback and relayed it to the company. Then we waited to see what their response would be.

Arriving back in Cincinnati, I turned my cell phone on as the plane landed on the runway. Immediately, my phone chimed with a missed call and a voicemail waiting for me. The voicemail was from the recruiter. In the message he told me that all my conditions, or requests, had been met. All of them! I again found myself in a state of shock. Since all the requests had been agreed to, I knew this was my next step. I realized where I was meant to be, so I accepted the offer with the company. Now I was left with the challenging task of trying to determine my next steps and how I would navigate such an early departure from my current company.

Upon completion of the background check and all the required paperwork being finalized with the new organization, I needed to provide a written notice to my current company. As expected, this did not go well. The company's leadership team were understandably frustrated with my quick departure from their organization and were even more irritated when they learned about the new company that I would be going to, because my next company was a competitor for some of their brands. However, one of my requests of the new organization was not to work on anything that would compete with my existing company. I did not want anyone to think I would take anything confidential or do anything that would harm my existing employer. However, within thirty minutes of providing my notice, I was told by my manager to leave the premises immediately. It was like a scene from a movie or television show. I boxed my items from my desk and carried them to the door as they escorted me out. It ended up being the only time in my career when I was physically escorted from a building. To make the situation even more challenging, I had driven a company car to work that day and had no way home. So I found myself outside the building on the sidewalk, with my box of items in my hands, waiting on my parents to come and pick me up.

While some would consider this moment humiliating, I saw it as confirmation of my decision. I knew at that moment that my decision to depart the company was the correct one to make. I knew that what was waiting for me was better than what I was in, and I needed to trust God that all the paths had aligned to this moment for a reason. I was headed for something greater, and this would turn out to be true over the next several years for my family and my career.

As you navigate your career, realize that not every role you take will end up being what you thought it would be. You will make mistakes along the way for various reasons. You might take a role at a company, like I did, because you are out of work and need to make money to pay the bills. But this doesn't have to be where you stay. Use your contacts and your network to help you resolve your mistakes. The power of networking in my career has been much larger than I ever anticipated it would be. These connections can be a lifeline to you in times of challenge. Build your network early, and continue to focus on making and enhancing those connections throughout your career. Also, have faith and know that you will end up where you are meant to be! Sometimes, it just takes a little longer to get there.

Finally, you are inevitably going to have moments in your life you are not proud of, but realize these are lessons you can use for personal growth. Additionally, you can use these experiences to help guide others so they can avoid the challenges you have had to face. I learned from my transitions to be bold in what I ask for, and I always remember that no job or career in the business world is worth any long-term separation from my family.

Taking Care of Yourself Is a Priority

Do you find yourself overrun by work, family obligations, and household tasks? Have you maintained a focus on your health and wellbeing, or has that taken a back seat to the other needs in your life? With work, being a parent, and various obligations, it is easy to run out of time and energy to really focus on your health and wellbeing. At this point in my life, I had come to a crossroads with getting my family and my career in a good place while my personal health had declined as I had again put on quite a bit of weight. In this chapter, I'll share about my surgical weight loss journey and the new activities I grew to really enjoy.

After being back in Ohio for several months, we had moved out of my in-laws' house and into our new home. I began my new job, and everyone settled into a routine. Things were going very well for us, professionally and personally for our family. While life was never without challenges, things were good. However, for me, I needed to focus on a change in my health. My weight was now the highest it had ever been, and I was miserable with myself, despite having a good job and everyone in the family doing well. So I needed to make a change.

I had been on so many different weight loss journeys throughout my life. I had done Diet Workshop, Weight Watchers, Atkins, a general low-carb diet, etc., but nothing really worked for me as a longer-term solution. I needed to do something different, so I began to research weight loss surgeries. After looking at various options, I felt the best fit for me would be gastric sleeve surgery.

I met with various doctors and went to several information sessions to learn more. After a couple of months of research, I decided on a doctor that would do the surgery and would be mostly covered by insurance. While his presence and interactions were not the best, I felt like this was the best path forward for me. So I started the four- to six-month journey of preparing for a possible surgery. Part of the long process toward surgery included meeting with nutritionists, learning to diary my daily intake, meeting with psychiatrists, and showcasing to the doctors and nurses at the practice that I could be trusted to lose weight postsurgery. Unfortunately, my journey with this doctor did not go fully as planned.

During the process, my chosen doctor left his practice, and I was left to start the process all over again. Thankfully, the current practice recommended a few different options for other doctors I could utilize. So I made an appointment with one of them as I was determined to move forward with the surgery.

The new doctor was great! I was thankful for his willingness to be updated on what I had already accomplished, and I appreciated his improved ability to connect with patients compared to the previous physician. After a couple of appointments, the new doctor mentioned that he was impressed with my progress. He even mentioned that, compared to the other patients he had seen from this other doctor, I was well on my way to surgery, and he was now prepared to set a date. I had not expected this news. I was nervous, but I was extremely excited to start the next phase!

The final preparation for surgery was upon me, and it was a challenging two weeks, but I was ready to take it on and accomplish the final phase. During the two weeks prior to surgery, almost everything was stripped away from my diet. I was only permitted to have sugar-free and carb-free soft foods. For example, the majority of my meals consisted of sugar-free Jell-O, carb-free yogurt, and protein powder mixed with water. While this would be completely fine postsurgery when I would be devoid of most cravings and hunger, and would barely be able to eat, this was prior to surgery, making it one of the most miserable time frames to live through. But I lost almost twenty pounds in those two weeks prior to surgery, and getting the final clearance to finally have the surgery helped soften the misery.

The surgery was a success, and I had no postsurgical issues that sometimes occur in patients. Over the next year, I lost over 150 pounds and started to enjoy some incredible opportunities with my family and for myself. I ran multiple 5K races, ran a 10K and a 5K in the same day, hiked the Himalayan Mountains in India, went zip-lining in San Juan with my family, and spent a lot of time with my kids on various rides in amusement parks. We had an incredible amount of fun as a family, and I was finally able to participate in activities I'd never imagined for myself. It was an incredible time, and the experiences were amazing! Of the ones mentioned, India was the most impactful on me personally. If you had told me two years prior to going on the trip that I would be hiking in the Himalayan Mountains, I would never have believed you.

At the time of my surgical weight loss journey, I was working for a company that partnered with a global charity that focused on the health and well-being of children all over the world. As part of the charitable work done by the organization, my company held what they called a Global Challenge every other year. The Global Challenge, sponsored by the company, was an extensive effort to raise money for the partnered charity and make an impact in different parts of the world. That year's challenge included raising money for kids in India to improve hygiene in some of the more remote areas of the country. As part of the challenge, the participants raised the money needed to complete necessary upgrades at the school, including building a new restroom and handwashing facility, repairing the outer walls of the school yard, painting the school's classrooms and buildings, and creating and planting a garden the school could use to grow fresh produce to help feed the kids throughout the year.

To be considered for the challenge, each employee had to submit an application that included their reasons for wanting to engage in the event, how they planned to train, and a commitment to raise a specific amount of money. All the money raised would be used to complete the tasks needed for the school. As a reward for raising the money and committing to doing the work at the school, the Global Challenge participants would be taken on a five-day trek through the Himalayan Mountains in northern India. Having been on my surgical weight loss journey for almost a year, I thought this would be an excellent next step for me to push myself and have a goal in place to continue my journey. I had learned throughout my life that having a detailed goal for myself was required for me to put in the necessary effort and focus to accomplish it. However, I realized that with my company having thousands of employees around the world and only about forty who would be selected to represent approximately twenty-five to thirty countries, the selection process odds were not in my favor. But I made the decision to apply anyway as part of my goal-setting process. Several months later, I was traveling for work and was sitting at a group dinner when I received an email from the Global Challenge team. In the email I was informed by the company that I had been accepted for the upcoming Global Challenge event in India. My coworkers around the table were all excited for me, but my nerves started to settle in. I was excited, but I was also nervous about my ability to complete this type of hike. I didn't even like to camp in my backyard. How was I going to survive five days trekking through the Himalayan Mountains with a backpack? Was I nuts? The next challenge would be to tell my wife that I would be headed to India for two weeks later in the year.

Once home from my work trip, I informed my wife of the upcoming trip. Now, my wife and daughter love to camp, while my son is like his dad and has determined that roughing it in a tent with no shower or air-conditioning is not remotely appealing. So informing them of the upcoming challenge would be a funny adventure. My son thought I was crazy, and my wife and daughter were annoyed because they knew I hated to camp. While they were as surprised as I was that I had been selected from all the people in the company, they were also excited for me because they had been by my side throughout my weight loss journey.

My extended family were also nervous and excited about me going on the trip, and they did a tremendous amount of work to help me raise the money needed for the challenge. We had various fundraising events, and many wonderful people showed up to help fund what was needed for the trip. For my training, I continued running but pushed myself to do farther distances, including the 10K and 5K races on the same day. As a side note, this is not something I recommend for someone who is new to running. Just do the half-marathon instead. I realize it is longer, but the gap between the two races is just enough to cool down and make the shorter 5K a miserable task. Looking back, I think I would have had more success just doing the half-marathon. Additionally, my family and I took some hiking trips to various locations to do some of the training together.

As the India trip drew closer, I used each Saturday leading up to the trip to do longer-distance hikes or biking to try and build up the endurance I would need. On Saturday mornings, I woke up and prepared my gear for a long hike. I included in my backpack several protein bars, bottles of water, and additional gear as needed, depending on the weather for the day. I woke up my wife before I departed and let her know I was heading out, and that I would call her when I was ready to be picked up. She always asked in what direction I would be heading, to which my normal response was, "I'm not sure." I knew she wasn't thrilled by the response, but she just shook her head and went back to sleep.

The reason I never knew in what direction I would be heading was because we lived at the top of a hill, and at the bottom of the hill was a bike path where I could either go toward Morrow, Ohio, or toward Loveland, Ohio. The bike trail in Ohio is an enormous path that ultimately takes you from the state's northern border to its southern border, making it a great place to hike a long distance. My most memorable hike was the very first one. I learned a valuable lesson on this very first hike from home.

On my first hike, I left the house early in the morning. The weather was warm and sunny, and there was a great breeze that made the shady path of the trail perfect for a long hike. I headed toward Morrow and enjoyed the walk along the tree-lined path beside the gently flowing Little Miami River. There were many people out enjoying the day. Some were on the trail with me riding their bikes, running, or walking, and others were in canoes making their way down the river. While enjoying the sounds of people and nature during the hike, I had to pay attention while on the trail, because when those on bikes got close, they either rang their bells or yelled out that they were coming up on the left, so I wouldn't step out in front of them.

After hiking for about four hours, I decided that it was time to call my wife and give her my general location. Unfortunately, I found myself in a valley with little to no cell phone service. So I left the path and took a side road that led out of the valley and up to the highway. After climbing the steep hill out of the valley, I called my wife and gave her the general area where I thought I could meet her. Almost an hour later, we ended up meeting near a small diner called the Country Kitchen Restaurant. While this was about eight miles by highway from our home, it was about thirteen miles in walking distance based on the path I had taken. For my first hike, this was a bit farther than I had planned to walk. I was exhausted and could barely feel my legs by the time she picked me up. After this first hike, I became a little better at planning my route and ensuring my wife had a decent place to collect me.

After all the training, it was time for the trip. I had done my best to prepare myself for the journey, and now it was time to go. I was nervous about whether I had done enough, but I was excited to go do something I'd never thought possible for myself. It was time to leave for India.

Of all the various types of training I had done for the trip, I'd learned that hiking was my favorite. Leaving the house early on a beautiful day, not generally knowing where the path would take me, was very liberating and peaceful. Not only was it great exercise for my physical health, but the mental clarity and calmness it provided was good for my overall wellbeing. I often miss those hikes, and my wife and I talk about doing some of those together. Now, it's just finding the time and the will to do them.

The other thing I learned during this phase of my life was the importance of setting clear goals and plans. If I commit to a goal or plan, I can accomplish it. When I don't have clarity on what I'm working toward, I find myself just existing. My wife and I just had this conversation this week. Our kids are now grown, and we find ourselves in a moment of just existing. It's time for some goal setting and vision planning so we know what we are working toward.

Doing the "Impossible": Stretching Beyond Self-Imposed Limits

Are you facing a situation in your career, or a personal challenge, that seems impossible? Do you know your physical and mental limits? Do you try to avoid going beyond those limits because anything more is out of the realm of your potential? This chapter focuses on a key moment in my life when I faced a challenge that was bigger than I'd ever thought was possible for me. In my mind, how could a fat guy from the relatively flat Ohio valley ever physically or mentally achieve trekking the Himalayan Mountains in northern India?

The trip to India was upon me. The fundraising had been completed, the necessary trekking gear had been secured, the travel itinerary had been booked, and it was time to leave. The first leg of the trip was to fly to New Delhi to meet the other Global Challenge participants and our guides. Flying from Cincinnati, I took a short and uneventful United Airlines flight to Chicago where I changed planes and airlines at O'Hare International Airport. Once in Chicago, I boarded the Air India flight out of the international terminal for the fourteen-plus-hour flight to New Delhi. This turned out to be an interesting flight!

Boarding the Air India flight was an experience in and of itself. The plane was not in the best condition as it looked quite old and worn down. The carpet was coming up in the corners, some of the ceiling panels were loose and hanging, and the headset in the seat pocket in front of me was not usable. I chuckled to myself as I took the headset out to look at it. When I lifted it out of the seat pocket, I saw that the left earpiece was broken and dangling by a wire. Needless to say, it was not going to provide much use for me during this flight. I ended up learning a couple of valuable international flight lessons on this trip, as I had never flown overseas before.

International flight lesson number one: Do *not* sit in the row behind, or anywhere near, the bulkhead.

The bulkhead row is where the mothers with babies sit to use the wall snap-on baby beds. The seat location where I was sitting near the bulkhead row ensured I was in full hearing distance of the screaming babies for the entire flight. Lesson learned.

International flight lesson number two: Do *not* try to get up and navigate to the restroom during the night hours on the plane. To be fair, this could be an Air India-specific issue, but I was shocked to see so many women sleeping in the aisles of the plane. When I had to go to the restroom, I was forced to step over many women laying in the middle of the aisle, just so that I could reach the facilities. While the flight attendants navigated this with ease, I was more challenged. Partway down the aisle, I decided to just give up and returned to my seat as, at any time, if we were to hit a pocket of any turbulence at all, I would have been stepping on someone's wife or mother. I decided that it just wasn't worth it and I would wait until daytime arrived on the plane.

International flight lesson number three: Ahead of the flight, learn the potential food menu and how the flight attendants may ask for your meal preference. After several rounds with the flight attendant asking me "Veg, no veg" at a very rapid pace, and having no idea what she meant, I finally realized the options were either vegetarian or with meat. I unwisely chose the "no veg" option and got to experience mutton. I would have been better off going with the vegetarian option, but again, lesson learned: understand the potential menu ahead of time, and be prepared!

My seatmates during the flight from Chicago to New Delhi also offered a fun experience. If the older gentleman sitting next to me wasn't sleeping on my shoulder or stretching with his armpit in my face, his wife was audibly belching. I'm not sure if it was a medical condition, but it was constant—multiple times per hour, every hour, as long as she was awake. The belching was so loud that there were multiple occasions when the mothers with the screaming babies in front of us turned around and gave me nasty looks. I guess the somewhat overweight guy in the row was the most likely culprit in their minds. Fun flight!

Now in New Delhi, after disembarking from my flight, I was greeted by our guides and loaded into a hired car. The car took me to the hotel where I was able to get checked in, and I was provided with the time to meet the rest of the group later that afternoon for our trip's official kickoff meeting. Since it was late morning and the meeting was in the afternoon, there was really no time to rest. So I dropped my luggage in my room and met with the group. I had finally officially started on the journey.

After dinner with the group and some much-needed rest from the long travel time, our full group headed out early from the hotel in New Delhi. We boarded a large tour-style bus and headed to the train station. While it was only a short trip on the bus to the train station, the station brought an opportunity to learn a valuable life lesson.

Once off the bus, we all gathered our gear and headed to the train station's security checkpoint. Much like at an airport, we had to place our bags on the belt and proceeded through the metal detector. I was toward the back of the line of approximately forty people on our trip, so I had plenty of opportunities to see how the security process worked. I was also able to see how the interactions with locals played out in the security line. Surprisingly, the locals were very bold in how they approached the line. Instead of joining the end of the queue, as I would have anticipated, the locals walked to the front by the security scanner belt, physically knocked our people out of the way, placed their bags on the belt, and walked through without saying a word. I thought to myself, *OK, I see how this works now.* So, when it came time for me to put my stuff on the belt, up came a local person. The local bumped into me and attempted to knock me out of the way. To their surprise, I knocked them back out of the way and placed my stuff on the belt instead. Without a word, they looked at me and got behind me in line.

Lesson learned: Try your best to understand the local practices and expectations through observation and understanding, and act like a local. If you don't, be prepared to wait or take a back seat to someone else. No one is going to step in and help you. Help yourself!

The next four and a half hours on the train were amazing. Not because of the train, which was actually quite an interesting experience itself, but because of the views. The countryside outside of the larger city of New Delhi was absolutely beautiful! Although the city was a bit dirty and crowded, like most cities, the countryside was filled with wide-open green spaces and beautiful views. The train, as I mentioned, was an interesting experience. We were ticketed for first-class seats, but it was not what you are probably thinking. The seats were old and worn, and the bathroom had a hole in the floor where you could quite literally watch the railroad ties rush past below you as the train sped down the tracks. However, there was only one person per seat, and no one was standing in the aisle, which was more than I could have said for the various trains we passed while on the tracks. There were several trains going by, looking like those you would see on television, filled to their max standing capacity, with people hanging out on the sides and some on the top. It was quite a sight to see.

We finally arrived in Haridwar via train in the very early afternoon and switched to hired cars. Having hired cars for so many people almost looked like a train of a different variety once we were on the road, and with all of us having the same red bags provided for us for our gear, the cars were oddly uniform.

After departing the train station, we spent the next six or seven hours driving up to the Himalayan Mountains in the state of Uttarakhand. While the scenery was beautiful, the drive was very challenging as a passenger.

Getting out of Haridwar was a bit overwhelming to my senses as the roads were filled with cars, trucks, tuk-tuks, motorcycles with multiple family members on them, bicycles, people walking, and various roaming animals. Watching the driver go through Haridwar, I was reminded of being a kid and driving through the middle of town with my grandfather. My paternal grandfather, the over-the-road truck driver, was always driving through town like he was in a parade. Despite there only being the one stop sign in the village, he would honk at anyone he saw, waving his hands out the window while shifting gears, playing with the radio, and spitting tobacco in his spit cup. I was always amazed at his ability to do all these things at once. Now, I must admit, the driving wasn't stellar, but we never had an accident.

Navigating Haridwar was just like being with Pap; the hired car's driver was honking regularly, waving his hands out the window, shifting gears, and generally yelling at various people on the roads. Within our group in the car, I was the calmest in the group as I had had the most experience with this type of car ride. Once home, this was the first thing I told my dad. I told him, "Dad, I finally understand Pap. I know exactly where he should have lived."

Once out of the city, the roads became mountain roads and were quite narrow despite traffic going both ways, including trucks, and the roads twisted and turned as we made our way into the mountains. I could see the remnants of various mudslides on the roads and infrastructure, and I saw the challenges of maintaining these roads faced by the Indian government. I felt like I was on a reality TV show about dangerous roads. After six or seven hours of fun in the cars, we arrived at our next hotel and stayed for the night. Having been on a bus, a train, and in hired cars for the entire day, we were all exhausted and ready for bed.

The next day, we headed out in various cars again for about another five hours until we reached a school located in the mountains. Now, this was not the school where we would be volunteering. We would not arrive at that school until after the trek was completed. The school where we arrived on this day was our campsite for the night so that we could start our trek early the next morning.

For the night, we slept in tents scattered around the schoolyard located on the side of a mountain. Unfortunately, there was a heavy rainstorm overnight, and a small mudslide made its way through our campsite. At one point in the middle of the night, I felt like I was sleeping on a waterbed. My thin, self-inflating air mattress was rocking side to side as though it were floating on waves in the ocean. It turned out that this was when the mud was coming through, because the tent I was sleeping in was one of only two tents that were completely surrounded by four to five inches of mud the next morning. Thankfully, all my gear was inside the tent. This was not the case for the team members in the other tent, as one of them lost several key components that he would need for the trip, including his hiking boots.

The next morning after the storm, we gathered our gear and began our first day of trekking in the mountains. Each day, we left the site with only what we needed for the day's hike. Our tents and the remainder of our gear were loaded onto horses after we left the campsite. Then, around mid to late morning, the horses and guides carrying our tents and the remainder of the gear passed us on the trail. This allowed them to get ahead of us and set up for lunch. We eventually caught up and reached them around lunchtime. We took a rest to eat lunch and then set out again for the second portion of the day's hike. Around midafternoon, the horses and guides with all our gear passed us again to set up the campsite for the evening and start cooking dinner. The guides and crew on the trek were amazing! They had everything ready for us, and the food was really good. I had never liked Indian cuisine, but the food these guides prepared was unlike any other Indian food I had ever had. If I could get Indian food like this at home in the US, I would eat it more often. Additionally, the team that set up the site and made dinner sourced and boiled the next day's water for us. They cooled the water by placing it in a stream of cold snowmelt water that was flowing down from the upper portion of the mountain. It was amazing to see how the team did everything, and there was no way to thank them enough for how they took care of us on the trip!

On day one, we ended up hiking for about five hours up the mountain and then five hours back down again on another side. Day two was about three hours down, followed by seven hours up. Day three was like day two, three hours down and seven hours up. The final day of official trekking was about three hours up to our highest summit, Kuari Pass, followed by about seven to eight hours down to a village where the hired cars retrieved us. I would like to say I did the trek 100 percent on foot, but an issue on day two prohibited me from claiming that victory.

Waking up on day two was a tremendous challenge. I was still exhausted from the prior day's hike, trying to adjust to sleeping on the side of a mountain on a very thin self-inflating mattress, and trying to make sure I was well prepared for the day ahead. Unfortunately, on this day, I did not prepare myself well enough for the hike ahead. While I successfully maneuvered the hike for most of the morning, I started to slow down and really struggle as we got close to lunch. I was struggling to breathe, and I was getting a bit shaky. I needed to rest for a moment so I could finish the morning's hike, so I took a quick seat on a large boulder next to where we were walking.

As I was resting on the boulder, the doctor on the trip stopped to have a chat with me. She could see my hands were shaking, and she started to question my preparation and food intake for the morning. After she determined I had not eaten well enough to last the morning's hike, she gave me some glucose tablets and recommended that I focus on getting better hydrated. The doctor then recommended I utilize the horse to get to the lunch spot for the day so I could be better equipped for the afternoon hike. Although I did not want to utilize the horse out of embarrassment, I relented. So I got on the horse and took an extremely terrifying fifteen-minute ride to the day's lunch spot. I was able to finish hydrating, and I took in enough calories and protein to make the afternoon hike without any issues.

While I knew the moment on the horse was what I'd needed, I was embarrassed and felt like I had let myself down. I also felt like I had just showcased to the group that I had not prepared well enough for the trek. I was determined to not let this happen again for the remainder of the trip, and it would not. For the remaining trek days, I ensured I was preparing appropriately by having enough intake at breakfast to last through the morning. I also made sure to more frequently drink the water I had with me, and I realized that I must forgive myself for what had transpired on day two. If I focused too much on that one moment of need, I would not be mentally prepared for what remained.

The final trek day arrived, and a small number of us who were a bit slower with our hiking took off about thirty minutes ahead of the rest of the group. The morning was a bit chilly given our elevation, and the weather was misting rain which turned the mountain into a little bit of a muddy mess. This also caused the morning hike to be a bit slippery, slowing our progress; however, we were able to maintain a strong enough pace so that the second group caught up with us as we prepared to reach Kuari Pass. I made it. After months of preparation, I finally reached the top of our trek. I took several photos to ensure I would never forget this moment, and I sat for a bit to relax and enjoy the view while we were there. It was a powerful moment as we looked back on where we had come from on the trek and enjoyed a tremendous view. Unfortunately, we still had many hours of hiking left, so we didn't get to stay still for long.

We set off again and finished the remaining seven hours of hiking down the mountain to a local village where the hired cars were waiting to pick us up. Getting into the cars in the village was partially a relief because we got to sit somewhere comfortable and relaxing, but it was also a challenge due to the stench from having multiple trekkers in one car. The cars headed out and took us back to the hotel where we had stayed before we'd begun the trek. While dinner was already set up and waiting for us, my first task upon arrival at the hotel was to take a much-needed shower. After I finished getting cleaned up and changed into fresh clothes, I grabbed dinner with the team and headed off to bed.

The next morning, we woke up early and got in the hired cars to head back to Haridwar. The ride was about four or five hours back through the narrow curvy roads, but this was our last day in the mountains as we prepared for the next part of the trip: working at the school. We arrived in Haridwar that afternoon and decided as a group to head to a local market and then to the Ganges River for the evening ceremony.

After settling in at the hotel, I met up with some of the other team members and we took a car to a market near the Ganges River. The street at the market was narrow and lined with small shops along both sides. With lots of people on the street at the shops, and small scooters and motorcycles traversing through the crowds, the market was a touch overwhelming. However, the people were very nice and the fabrics in the shops were beautiful. I was enjoying looking at one of the shops from the street when I heard a bit of commotion going on behind me. It sounded like some people were starting to panic a little as I heard screams and the rustling of people moving quickly and possibly running, so I turned around. I was a bit concerned by what I saw, but I tried to stay calm and not make any sudden moves. There was a full-grown, massive bull making his way through the market. I backed up against the crowd at the shop where I had been browsing, but the bull was so close that I could reach out and touch him. I maintained my stillness and let him pass. He eventually made his way out of the market, and the sounds and hustle in the market returned to normal.

A short while later, we all met up again and headed to the river's edge for a ceremony that was about to begin. The river was fast-running, and it looked like it would be good for rafting. The edge of the river in this area was lined with concrete steps that had metal poles with chains on them that led into the water. At first, I was confused by the poles and chains, until I saw some of the locals utilizing the poles to get into the river to bathe themselves. I was impressed by their bravery to enter such a fast-running river, as it would have made me nervous about whether I could keep my footing. We finished our walk across the bridge over the river to join the crowd for the ceremony.

The dusk ceremony is called the Ganga Aarti and is held at the edge of the river. It was beautiful, and the crowd of people at the ceremony was massive. It was October and one of the key times of the year for the ceremony. As dusk set in and the ceremony progressed, fires lit up the area while the holy chants were spoken. Several of our team members joined in on the ceremony by releasing lit diyas down the rushing river. The river, now lit by what seemed like hundreds of diyas, rushed by with a serene beauty. The team finished releasing their diyas, and we headed back to the hotel.

The next morning, after grabbing breakfast at the hotel, we got back into the cars and headed out of the city to a local village school. The drive was beautiful and scenic, and watching several motorcycles go by filled with families was impressive. One motorcycle went by with a family of four on board.

Upon arrival at the school, we got out of the cars and made our way to the schoolyard's entrance. As we entered, the kids were lined up on each side of the path to greet us with their teachers. Our goal while at the school was to help clean up, paint the classrooms, repair and paint the exterior walls, finish up the new restroom and handwashing facilities, and build and plant a garden for the school to grow food which they would use to feed the students. We quickly divvied up our tasks among the team and got started on our work.

I had the opportunity to work on the exterior wall and a little on the garden. The exterior wall caught my attention for a couple of reasons. First, there were shards of glass cemented onto the top of the wall like spears jutting out of concrete. This was to keep the wild animals, like leopards, out of the schoolyard and ensure the safety of the children while they were at school. Second, there were repairs that needed to be made to the lower parts of the wall. There was a very large hole that needed patched up. When we inquired about the repair, we were informed that it was needed to ensure crocodiles couldn't get into the schoolyard during the rainy season. The school had lost some enrollment due to the challenges with safety for the children, and the issues we were meant to address were critical for the school.

While working on the wall was a challenging task in the heat of the day, it was a source of pride. Knowing that what I was working on was directly related to keeping the kids safe was fulfilling. I spent that day and the next painting the interior and exterior of the massive concrete wall and helping to plant vegetables in the newly created garden. During the day, we broke for lunch and interacted with the kids in the school. We played games, taught them about the importance of washing their hands, and got to enjoy seeing their faces light up with the various changes being made at the school.

After our second day of working at the school, we finished all the projects we had set out to complete, and we headed back to the hotel in Haridwar. After our final night in Haridwar, we went to the train station and made our way back to New Delhi where we spent one final night before departing for home.

Looking back on the Global Challenge trip to India, making the summit on Kuari Pass during the final day of trekking remains something I will never forget. I spent months physically preparing for the trek, but I don't think I was mentally prepared for what the trip would truly mean to me. I never thought I would be capable of trekking the Himalayan Mountains, or that I would have the opportunity to work at a school in a remote village on the other side of the world helping others, but I did it. I learned that I could truly do whatever I wanted to do if I focused and really worked at it. All it took was determination, preparation, and a willingness to be open to new things.

Finally, there are so many things we take for granted within the US. Our kids generally have schools that are not to the level of disrepair or challenges that you may find in other parts of the world. Kids in the US typically aren't sitting in school worried about whether a crocodile will be in the schoolyard when they head out for recess. Our schools aren't usually concerned about the need to grow food to feed the students in their care. We are very blessed as a country, and we should utilize our time and abilities when we can to help others who struggle with some of these basics.

I would like to thank the organization I worked for, my coworkers who were on that incredible journey with me, and the guides and staff who were with us to make everything possible! I could not have done it without you, and it is a moment in my life that I will cherish forever!

Now, take a moment to think about something you may be avoiding because you think it isn't possible. Is it truly not something you can do, or have you placed this limitation on yourself because you are unsure if you can accomplish it? I love the quote from the great Wayne Gretzky: "You miss 100 percent of the shots you don't take." Therefore, try to accomplish what you think is out of reach. You may just surprise yourself, just like I did at the top of a mountain on the other side of the world.

Listening to God's Voice, Standing Up for Yourself, and Trusting God's Vision

Have you experienced moments in your life or career when you knew a change needed to be made, but the timing just didn't feel right? Perhaps you have experienced a time when something was told to you about your career or your next steps, but they didn't come to fruition, and because you didn't have it in writing, there was nothing you could do. Or your company restructured the business, and your entire future potential career progression was wiped out. What do you do, or what have you done, in these scenarios? In this chapter, I will share about each of these moments in my career, what decisions I made, and how each led me to a new learning about my faith and leadership lessons.

Back in Cincinnati and now having worked at my company for about six years, the organization decided to reorganize. This was nothing new for the company as they had been known to restructure the business every two to three years to meet changing needs. Unfortunately, my department would not be exempt during this change.

The boss I had worked for over the last few years, and one whom I greatly appreciated, had been removed from the organization when his position was eliminated. With his position no longer existing, the entire department was broken up and placed into another portion of the company. My department's focus was, and was intended to be, externally focused on driving the business by ensuring we understood what the shopper wanted and how to effectively drive the retailer's performance. As part of the new structure, the separation we had historically had from the internally focused teams was now gone. Additionally, there was no longer anything above my role for me to grow into. It was time to start looking elsewhere if I wanted to continue my long-term growth within the function I enjoyed and the one I had built my entire career around.

Once I made the decision to start looking, I felt an overwhelming sense of a message to hold. I felt as if God was nudging me to stay within the company a bit longer. I was not sure why I was meant to stay, but I held off on searching for a new role. Months passed by, and I continuously heard "Hold," but then it changed.

After several months of adjusting to the new structure and fighting to maintain our externally focused priority, I finally felt a release to move forward with a search. Interestingly, I did not need to even put in one application. Within a few days of the release to move on, I was contacted by a company looking for me to potentially lead their insights team in the Cincinnati market. While there was currently leadership in place, the current leader was looking to be promoted, and they wanted to set up a backfill for when their promotion occurred. So I made the decision that I was going to look at the opportunity seriously.

I met with the other company's HR department, their local leaders, and the head of the department for the US business. All were aligned with me as a hire to be the future backfill for the team, or so I was told during the hiring process. Therefore, I provided my notice to my current organization and departed on good terms with the leadership team. I took a role with the new organization in a slight step down under the agreement that I would move into the leadership role once the current lead was promoted; however, while I had a verbal agreement to the future role, I did not get it in writing. This was my mistake that I would learn to not repeat in the future.

Now working for the new company, I enjoyed getting to meet the team and start developing them in new skills they had not been able to learn yet. I was also able to start meeting with our customer contacts and showcase the value I could bring to the selling relationship. The company was a good company with amazing brands, along with some great people. Unfortunately, it did not work out for me in the long term.

After a few months of working on the team, I saw the influence of specific leaders and their goals within the local team. They had a leadership style which they felt was the most effective, and they pushed other leaders within the office to do the same. If you didn't align with their leadership style, not only would they challenge you at every turn, but they would go to your leadership and provide negative feedback. One of the most interesting and influential moments of dealing with this scenario was a conversation with our key customer. Following a meeting within the corporate office of our key customer, our contact pulled me aside after a key meeting we had with them and asked me a very direct question. The customer asked me, "Why are working for them?" They went on to tell me that specific leadership within my new company was too inwardly focused and didn't care about the customers' needs, and this person again pressed me on why I would want to work there. They even encouraged me to get out. While this caught me off guard, I took it as a challenge to help drive change within the team. I wanted this person to see what our team could be as a resource for their company. I wanted them to see us evolve, and I hoped that I could help be the catalyst for the change.

I spent the next several months continuing to push for a new working style within the local office. While I butted heads with the other leadership, I continued to press on by utilizing a different style. I worked on showcasing that we could get more accomplished, while improving our reputation with our customer at the same time, by modifying our approach. Unfortunately, what I did not have visibility to was the feedback loop that was working around me to undermine what I was working toward. Therefore, what I was pursuing ultimately failed.

About nine months into the role at the new company, the existing leader of my team got promoted as planned and moved on. This was when I found out about the alternate feedback loop that had been going into the corporate office. While I'd had a verbal agreement and understanding of my next role, it did not come to fruition and the organization proceeded to hire someone from outside the company to take on the leadership role for my team.

The new leader hired for the team was quite good. I appreciated her style and quickly believed she would be a good fit for the team. However, I was concerned for her in that I didn't believe she truly knew what she was getting into at the company. I could see her style would also not fit with the other local leadership, and I had doubts that anyone hiring her would inform her of the agreement they'd made with me during my hiring process about a year prior. So I decided to focus on doing my job to the best of my ability, and I did not inform her of my situation. I felt it would be inappropriate for me to treat her poorly or to bring her up to speed on something that could have potentially made her feel bad about the situation or make her feel sorry toward me. While I did not know what had or hadn't been shared, I determined it was not my place to do so.

A couple of months had gone by, and the new leader and I were working well together. She allowed me to do my job as I saw fit and allowed me to continue to help the team in various ways, but I started to see her getting a bit frustrated with the local office situation regarding the other leadership. This was when she pulled me aside and wanted to understand a little more about how things were progressing for me in the company.

I allowed her to start the conversation, and she proceeded to let me know that she had recently been brought up to speed on why I had been hired. She was very curious why I had never said anything to her, but she understood and appreciated my feedback when I fully debriefed her on the full background. She mentioned she was quite surprised to hear what had happened to me as she would never have guessed that from how I had been treating her from the beginning. I took this as a compliment. I fully believed it would have been inappropriate for me to treat her poorly or try to influence her perspective on the company from the beginning with my specific situation. I appreciated working with her, and I thought she felt the same way about me. Her main concern was understanding how she could help me. We had some good conversations about the next steps and what would be best for me personally, but ultimately, I ended up parting ways with the company.

After having been with the organization for just over a year, my cell phone rang early one morning while I was sitting in the office. I answered, and I was surprised to hear the voice of a senior leader from my old company. This leader mentioned that the structure had been reverted to its previous state, and he wanted to see what it could look like for me to return to the company.

After our conversation, the new leader over my former department reached out, and within the next week, I was hired back to the company as the new head of insights. Although the role had been intended to be filled locally in the area around that office, it was agreed that I would fill it from a remote position halfway across the country. This being before the COVID-19 pandemic, I was surprised with the opportunity, and I was beyond grateful for the chance to do the role.

Looking back on this time in my career and the changes that occurred, I now understand the various reasons why these events unfolded the way they did. My time of "hold" at the company following the initial restructure allowed me to see what was inherently wrong with the structure and how I would do things differently. This timing also put me in a place at a new organization that allowed me to appreciate what I had in my prior company and learn two key lessons: how not to lead an office and customer relationship, and how to work with others despite potentially awkward situations.

The other benefit of the move to a new company, amid the many structure changes, was that it provided me with an opportunity in my old organization that would not have been permitted had I stayed through the reorganization. If I had not left, I know I would not have been permitted to lead the broader insights function nationally from Cincinnati. I would have been forced to relocate, which was not a possibility for me at that time given the ages of my kids. I did not want to move them during high school, and this provided me with career growth opportunities without the personal costs to my kids.

Finally, I learned a valuable lesson through the restructuring process about all the time in my career I had spent dedicated to my depth of expertise within my function. I spent so much time developing in depth that I lacked the breadth needed to ensure longer-term viability in the marketplace. Therefore, as you progress through your career, find opportunities to cross-train into other functions when those moments become available. This can help you have additional experience and skill sets to more effectively navigate corporate restructuring. While a single experience-focused progression can allow you to build depth, it can leave you with few options should the organization deprioritize your function within the business.

IMPACT OF LEADERSHIP COACHING

Over the course of your career, have you ever considered externally sourced coaching? Or has all your coaching and mentoring been from those inside your organization? I found myself desiring more understanding of my capabilities as a leader and how I could shape my skills to further impact both my organization and my career path. While my company offered a 360-degree feedback process I could use, it was run by the human resources department and results were shared within the leadership team. Therefore, all participants in the process were contacted by HR with their input being captured by people who knew them. Although this process may work for some, I wanted a different experience. I wanted the ability for my participants to have a fully anonymous feedback loop to me. A process where the participants did not know the person collecting the data, and where they felt secure knowing what they shared could never have any impact on them at all. For me, I wanted an unbiased moderator to avoid any industry spin or influence on the results that would be shared with me. In this chapter, I will share the details about my process with executive coaching and the influence it has had on both my career and thought processes in key scenarios.

Moving back to my old organization a little over a year after leaving was a humbling experience. While there were many who were happy to see me return and engage with me as if I had never left, many others made sure each interaction with me included subtle reminders that they would not forget I had departed the company. This diminished over time but kept me a bit nervous in some meetings, holding me back from truly stepping up into my new position. I knew I needed to adjust my work style and interactions with others, but I still held back. I needed to change, and I had an idea.

During my review sessions with my direct leader, I asked for feedback on what else I should be doing to increase my influence. I was trying to see how I was being viewed by him and the company, but his responses were typically, "Keep doing what you are doing." While I really enjoyed working for my manager, I needed more, so I made the decision to approach an executive coach outside of the company. She was a tremendous person who had extensive experience with coaching leaders and helping others identify their strengths. Her first recommendation was to have a 360-degree feedback process completed so we would have a starting point.

For my 360-degree process, I gave her fifteen names of various people both inside and outside the company. These included a mix of people above me, at the same level, and those whom I had or was currently managing.

Warning: If you are not open to diving deep into others' perceptions of you, then this type of process is not for you. A 360-degree feedback process can be very challenging! By having my coach interact with these contacts in one-on-one conversations with a promise of anonymity, full transparency was achieved. If you don't go into it understanding there will be highly critical feedback of you, then you could be very hurt by the emotionally taxing process.

Once my coach completed all fifteen of the interviews, she compiled them into larger bucketed themes, and we connected in person to review her binder of quotes. We started the in-person review process with me reading the first section, highlighting areas I agreed or disagreed with, and then discussing what I had read in each of the sections. While I was reading each section, I saw her sitting across the table, on occasion bending down a bit, and checking to see how I was doing. I may have surprised her a bit because I was not having any feelings of hurt or bitterness toward the harder comments I was reading, but rather, I was excited. In this moment, I was so excited to get exposure to the opportunities that any other potential emotions took a back seat. I almost felt free. I felt like I was being given permission to do things in the company where I had been holding myself back. It was a very liberating process for me!

Coming out of this meeting with my coach, I had some solid themes I could build on. I learned that I needed to engage in intentional vocalization, I needed to push my agenda within the company, I had to embrace the unknown aspects of the business, and I needed to create and commercialize my personal brand. So what did these mean, and how did they shift others' perceptions of me over time?

Intentional vocalization was my personal branding of a "speak up" mentality. There was a perception by others that, when in larger meetings, I was either uninterested in the topic at hand, not paying attention, or that I lacked the experience to engage. It was a bit surprising to me that what I perceived as meeting etiquette was being thought of in this way. Within meetings, I had always held myself to the rule of thumb that I would speak when something needed to be said. If others had already made the point, I was not going to interject or repeat the thought just so they could hear me speak. This was a mistake! While I maintained my effort to avoid duplicative commentary, I started to ensure that I added on to the main thoughts or points I agreed with in the meeting. If I left a meeting without saying anything during the body of the session, I would have failed at my goal. Therefore, I began to intentionally look for ways to interact with others in meetings. While to me this felt like a minor shift, the feedback after six months was very positive. Additionally, I found myself better prepared for meetings as I often spent time pregaming the topics to see how else I could engage. This started to impact my confidence in very positive ways.

The second theme was to push the agenda of the organization to include my priorities as a leader. I had very clear goals for my personal team and the broader department, but I had been waiting for permission to pursue them. I had been waiting for an official go-ahead from my leadership team, but I needed to view my hiring into the position as my green light. If the leadership team didn't believe I could handle what needed to be done or didn't believe in my vision, they wouldn't have put me in the position. So I started to be bolder in my decision-making and intercompany interactions. I set up meetings with key stakeholders to talk through key topics and showcase why we needed to adjust what we were doing. I actively started working to build the network of support for changes I wanted to enact. This also went over quite well with the team over the next six months. Not only did I engage and develop a support group for my changes, but the feedback went from a desire for me to push the agenda to a desire for me to ensure I closed the loop on my ideas and changes. They were bought in, and now they wanted to see how they would turn out.

Embracing the unknown was born from feedback that, while I was very well-known and regarded in my half of the company (sales), the other half (marketing) was hit or miss. There were some contacts in the marketing organization with whom I had engaged and gotten to know, but there were many more I needed to influence to fully enact my vision. I needed to embrace this challenge and start connecting more deeply with key contacts on the marketing side of the business. One of the ways I tackled this was through the consumer insights group within marketing.

Since I worked in shopper reporting through sales, the consumer insights group reporting through marketing was a separate silo I needed to penetrate. So I began to actively engage with some of the key contacts on the consumer insights team. I connected with them a few times a year to try and share ideas and come up with better ways of working together, but there was always a hurdle there. It started to feel a little like running into a wall. I needed to change tactics if I was going to be successful.

As time progressed, a need for understanding during COVID handed me a golden opportunity for integration. Before everything shut down in the country, I started compiling a plan of learning. I worked with our team to understand what they would want to know and how this could impact shopping. Additionally, we laid out plans for where we could source this information. I used this plan to start aligning with the consumer group. I wanted to understand what their needs would be and how they would go about obtaining the data. As it turned out, the week we aligned on all the topics and sources, the world changed. We finalized our plans on Thursday, and by Saturday, the US was in shutdown mode.

Now, since we had a road map in place, we enacted it immediately and got working on gathering the needed information. Within days, we were learning about what we needed to do in the marketplace. Within weeks, the shopper and consumer teams were working deeply together to drive business knowledge and next steps. A year later, we looked back at what we'd predicted for the business in those first couple of weeks, and we found that we had been incredibly accurate! We'd shifted how we worked, and it had resulted in great collaboration. Additionally, the information we were compiling was leading in the marketplace. Our key stakeholders in the company were able to give what we were learning to their customers, and we were quickly getting invited to larger engagement sessions that would help shape the business and our relationships.

My final pillar to pursue was to create and commercialize my personal brand. This one took me some time to put together. I needed to really ensure I understood how I wanted to be perceived in the organization and how I wanted people to think of me when I was not in the room. So I leaned on what I thoroughly enjoyed doing and areas that gave me strength when I was engaging with them.

The key theme I wanted people to remember about me was that I coached and developed others through challenging situations to help surprise and delight their key stakeholders. The pillars of the brand I wanted to relay included people thinking about my ability to fix broken processes, my skills in distilling complex information into understandable pieces, my focus on strategic change, my role as a credible source of information that was trustworthy and consistent, and my ability to often surprise and delight others with the information they were being provided.

After creating my branding, my coach started to pressure test it among the same folks who had provided the 360-degree feedback, and the response was overwhelming to me. While I did not get to relay my brand directly to these coworkers, the quotes I received were, in some respects, validation that I was doing the right things. Some of the comments were: "These are spot-on," and, "He's always, always, always done this." This was exciting for me, as I could continue to use this as a blueprint for years to come.

From the branding work I completed, the Mr. Fix-It label stuck with me. My senior leadership contact, seeing the impact I was having within my role, asked me to connect with him directly about a key topic. As it turned out, there were some challenges within one of the budgets he was influencing. He needed someone to dive into the key details and determine the next steps to resolve the issues being experienced. I agreed to jump in, and I would report back once I had completed my review.

I spent several weeks gathering information, communicating with the budget holders, and gaining insight into the line items. This budget turned out to be a very complex piece of work. Not only were there millions of dollars in line items included, but there were also multiple parts of the organization responsible for funding and approving the key pieces. This budget needed more people resources to manage it, and it needed a well-documented process for how it should be managed each year.

I reported back on the findings and what the needs were in a clear and concise manner, thinking my portion of this would be over after my report. However, that assumption proved to be incorrect. Upon completion of the meeting to review the process recommendations and key findings, I was told that the plan sounded great and that I should let him know what I would need to implement it as I moved forward with ownership of the budget. I was quite surprised by the assignment of ownership, but I was also looking forward to getting my hands into a new area of business that was more closely aligned with my college degree in accounting. While challenging, this was a great opportunity for me to learn even more about the business and capabilities within the marketplace, and it proved to be quite valuable to me personally over the next two years.

After my executive coaching process ended, I saw great success at work. I was learning a lot of new things, but I was also seeing the positive impacts from the changes I was making. Unfortunately, an upcoming organizational leadership overhaul and a personal health emergency permanently changed my path with this company.

The impact of the executive coaching process was immediate and long-lasting on my career, and I highly recommend this to anyone in a leadership position. However, don't do it unless you are 100 percent ready to hear the outcome.

Finally, if you are a leader of leaders, do not force your team to undergo a 360-degree feedback process unless they are ready to receive feedback. Forcing a leader to undergo the process can backfire. If forced, the leader will be unlikely to listen to the feedback, and the team members who provided the feedback won't see any change. This can result in resentment from the leader who was forced, and low morale among those who participated.

LEARNING FROM
OTHERS' MISTAKES

L et's think about scenarios in your life when you've placed yourself in someone else's care. This could be a taxi driver, an airline pilot, a train conductor, or even a medical professional. Have you had a moment when you've given information to one of these types of people that is key to your survival, and you have been ignored? Were they taking an unnecessary risk, or did they just feel like they knew better? Or were they too busy to be bothered by what you had to say? In this chapter, I'll share a moment in my life when a medical professional determined he already knew everything he needed to know about the situation, and he decided to ignore the details I provided to him about what was happening. His decision to ignore me almost killed me.

COVID hit in 2020, and I was spending my time diving deep into key areas of insights for my company so we could plan strategy and understand the best path forward regarding our brands. This was an incredible time of collaboration in the organization as we were experiencing many more connections and shared projects between the shopper and consumer teams. Additionally, the shopper and consumer groups were being brought into leadership meetings together to provide input and, on occasion, to present key learnings in tandem. The historic challenges with silos between our two teams coming into 2020 had taken a back seat, and we were doing more than ever together, which resulted in a more well-rounded understanding of the business.

While work was progressing well, my personal health was becoming a challenge. I started having severe pains in my stomach which resulted in me curling up in a ball on the floor for about an hour during each episode. I had been dealing with these pains once or twice a year for a few years. While I had been to the ER previously for this issue, there had never been any answers provided as to the cause. Unfortunately, they started to increase in frequency and duration, so I made the decision to finally find out what was truly causing the pain. After several tests with specialists, it was determined that my gallbladder needed to be removed, and it needed to be done soon.

Unfortunately, with COVID causing major challenges in hospitals across the country, getting surgery was going to be a challenge. Luckily, a date opened in October and the surgery was scheduled, so I began my prep with the surgeon and the day arrived.

Since this surgery was considered an outpatient procedure, the check-in process and surgery were relatively routine. After the surgery, I woke up in the recovery room and the discharge process started immediately. With COVID rules in place, my family was not permitted in the building and was required to wait in the car throughout the entire process. Therefore, once it was time for me to be discharged, the hospital brought someone to my room, and they held my arm while I walked to the entrance so my family could pick me up. While I hated having to be pushed in a wheelchair, I was quite surprised by the hospital's method of escorting me out of the building. Since I had recently woken up from the surgery, I was still lightheaded and struggled to maintain a straight line while walking out the door to the car. Once outside, I saw surprised looks on my family's faces as they hopped out of the car to further assist the hospital staff with getting me down the sidewalk.

Over the next few days, all proceeded as planned with my recovery; however, something began to feel a little off. I began to sweat profusely at the slightest exertion, and I was having quite a bit of pain in my stomach on a regular basis. With a postsurgery appointment with the doctor coming up soon, I decided to deal with the pain by taking some over-the-counter medication. Unfortunately, the pain continued to progress.

Thursday arrived, a week and a half after my surgery, and I went to the doctor's office for my follow-up appointment. The nurse took my vitals, and I explained the challenges I had been having, so she updated my information and told me the doctor would be in momentarily.

The doctor and his student came into the room. I relayed to the doctor the same information I had shared with the nurse about the pain, sweating, and not feeling well overall. Because I had noticed some white material on the surgical wound while I was at home, I proceeded to ask him if I could potentially have an infection. The doctor asked me to stand, raise up my shirt, and let him look at the surgical wound. By simply looking at the wound, the doctor told me there was no infection and that all looked good. I asked about the pain, and he blew it off, telling me to go home and rest and call back if I got any worse. I felt as though he believed I just wanted pain medication, which was not the case. I always try to avoid taking pain medication unless it is absolutely necessary, as most pain medications tend to make me nauseous. I left the doctor's office feeling frustrated and like I was overreacting.

The next day, Friday, I was working from home like normal, given the COVID conditions in the world. Unfortunately, I was now feeling even worse than before. The sharp pains had gotten more pronounced, and I'd struggled to sleep the night before. Additionally, I was feeling nauseous, but I was still trying to make it through my work meetings for the day. As I sat through my meetings at my desk in our basement, the pain continued to progress. With the level of pain I was now experiencing, I knew I would not be able to make it through the rest of my workday. Therefore, I sent a message to my boss and let him know I was not well and would be canceling the remainder of my meetings.

After contacting my manager, I shut down my computer and started walking up the stairs to the main floor of the house so I could rest on the couch. Climbing the steps got harder and harder, resulting in horrible stomach pain. If I had been asked by a nurse to rank my pain at that moment, it would have definitely been a ten. I finally made it to the top of the steps as my wife and daughter were getting ready to walk out the door to go to the store. My daughter, a college freshman at the time, turned to me and her expression looked a bit panicked. She and my wife asked me if I was OK. My normal response was always, "I'm fine. I'm just going to lie down for a little while." But that was not what came out of my mouth on that day. I looked at them and told them, "You need to take me to the ER."

As this type of response was highly unusual for me, they both instantly became concerned and helped me to get inside the car. Once we arrived at the ER, I signed in at the desk and took a seat in the waiting room area. Again, with COVID rules in place, neither my wife nor my daughter were permitted to come inside the building with me.

I went through triage, and I was taken to a bed inside the ER. Once in the emergency room bed, I brought the staff up to speed on everything that had been happening. While they offered me some pain medication to help reduce the pain I was obviously feeling, I refused. I let them know that I would not take anything until they could tell me what was causing the severe pain. The ER doctor sent me for an X-ray and began various testing. In the meantime, my daughter was permitted to come to the room now that I had been settled into a designated space. My daughter was going to keep track of me and keep my wife updated as she needed to head to work.

After the first test results came back, the head of the ER entered my room and let me know that the X-ray showed a fluid buildup within my abdomen. They were not yet sure what was going on, but I would need to be admitted for further testing. She asked me if there was anything I needed, so I relented and asked her if she could have some pain medication provided to me. The doctor seemed quite shocked. She asked me, "You haven't been given anything?" I told her that, up until that point, I had been refusing. I then explained what had happened the day prior at the surgeon's office. The doctor's shock shifted to what looked like anger. She verified with me. "You saw the surgeon yesterday?" I replied with a yes, and she said, "I will take care of this. I will order the meds, and the nurse should be in shortly. I'm going to go call the surgeon." I almost felt a little bad for the surgeon at this point because this doctor was clearly not happy with the situation, but at the same time, I was starting to get a little concerned and I was now wondering what she wasn't telling me. The doctor departed my room, and the nurse came in to provide the pain medication that had been ordered. Next, I was admitted, and I was moved to an upper floor of the hospital for the night.

Once they moved me into a room, the hospital team came in and took a blood sample for testing. My blood work showed that my white blood cell count was high, so they started me on a round of antibiotics. Tests, IV bags, and antibiotics continued for the entire next day on Saturday. I was doing OK by late afternoon, so my wife departed and headed home to prepare for work while my daughter stayed behind for a little while longer. Within an hour after my wife had left the hospital, I took a drastic turn. The pain escalated again and started causing me to vomit. My daughter rushed out of the room in search of help and quickly returned with the nurse. The nurse, who had been taking care of me for most of the day, noticed my drastic change and immediately called the doctor. Unfortunately, she was not able to get in contact with the doctor, so she sent me down for another test and said she would get the doctor's signature on my way there.

The test was completed, and I was sent back to my room. When the hospital transport person took me back to my room, I noticed that my wife had returned with my daughter and that the doctor was already in the room along with a couple of other hospital workers. I was not sure who the others were, but the feeling in the room had taken a turn. I felt like I was nineteen again in the hospital with the nurse who wouldn't talk to me anymore. Something had shifted. It was now after 9:00 p.m. on Saturday night, and my room was packed with medical staff.

They wheeled my bed into the room, and the doctor started to talk about the test results from the scan I had just completed. This seemed quite fast. How could they already have the results? The doctor looked at my wife, my daughter, and then at me. He said, "Sir, I'm not trying to panic you, but if you were my family member, I would want you in the operating room right now. I need your authorization to put you on the table and go back in to see what is happening, and I need to do that immediately. Are you OK to proceed?"

I agreed. What else was I going to say? The doctor informed my wife and daughter that the surgery would take about ninety minutes, and that they would be kept updated on my progress. The hospital staff wheeled me back out of my hospital room and down to pre-op. The pre-op space was quite different, late on a Saturday night. The room was very dim with minimal lighting being utilized as it was mostly empty except for just a few staff and myself. It almost looked like only the emergency lighting was on. Laying on the hospital bed, I was given another IV line, paperwork to sign, and a rundown of what was coming. The original IV line started throbbing and my arm was beginning to swell, so the nurse resituated the line and finished getting me prepped for surgery. Finally, I was transported into the operating room and moved to the operating table, and I watched the bright white lights of the cold, bustling operating room of people fade to black.

In recovery, I woke up to find myself with tubes coming out of my mouth and nose, and I was unable to speak to anyone. The nurse realized I was awake and immediately came to me to bring me up to speed. She was very sweet and calming, but she let me know that the surgery had been much longer and more involved than had been planned. She told me that I had a tube in my throat to pump my stomach, and she said not to panic, that I would be OK. The doctor would bring me up to speed later.

Once the doctor came to speak to me, he informed me that the ninety-minute estimate for the surgery had turned into over three hours in the operating room. While he'd started by entering on the left side of my body to see what was going on, he'd been unable to locate the issue. He'd ended up needing to reopen my surgical wound from the gallbladder surgery the week prior. The surgeon told me that once he'd opened the existing wound site, the infection had started immediately spilling out, and that it took him almost an hour just to clean out the surgical wound and ensure all the infection had been removed. Apparently, when the surgical site had been closed during the original surgery, the site hadn't been fully cleaned, and it had ended up getting infected. The emergency surgeon also mentioned that he was quite happy that I had come into the ER when I had because, had they not performed the surgery at that time, I would likely not have made it. I had been extremely close to sepsis, and my pain and illness symptoms had occurred because my organs had been starting to shut down.

I spent several more days in the hospital to recover from the emergency surgery and get the infection out of my body. I was released to go home and was told to set up a follow-up appointment with the original surgeon. While I was not happy about going back to see him, I needed to. What I wasn't prepared for was what his nurse would say to me at the appointment.

After arriving for my follow-up appointment with the original surgeon who had removed my gallbladder, I was placed into a room and told that someone would be with me shortly. A few minutes later, a nurse came into my room. I recognized her right away because she was the nurse who had seen me in the follow-up appointment when I'd originally told the surgeon about my pain and symptoms. She looked at me and said, "How are you doing?

You look so much better than the last time you were here!" She was correct, I was definitely doing better than I had been at the last appointment. I chuckled at her comment and let her know I was feeling much better. Then she looked directly at me and said, "I was shocked when the doctor let you leave the office last time you were here. It was obvious you were very sick and that something wasn't right."

I sat there in a bit of shock at her statement, but I felt vindicated somehow at the same time. I wanted to thank her for validating what I had been going through, but I decided not to say anything. She finished what she needed to do and told me the doctor would be right in. After she left the room, I kept replaying what she'd said to me, and I started to get angry and frustrated. If the nurse had seen it, why had the doctor just ignored me? Had he really thought I was just trying to get pain medication? Or had he not cared whether I lived or died? While these were answers I would never get, I learned some valuable lessons.

A doctor is the leader of their office. What type of leadership was my doctor showing to his staff and trainees when he met with me? Was he too busy to stop and listen? Did he prejudge the situation and ignore the facts that were being presented to him? What caused him to make such a mistake?

As a leader, you must make sure you are open to hearing the full situation. You need to slow down, and ensure you take in all the facts to make an informed decision. While there are times when a quick decision based on what you know is warranted, there are other more critical inflection points that require you to slow down and do a full evaluation of the situation. Don't hurt your company or your team members, or potentially someone else, because you can't be bothered to take a moment and hear all the facts!

CHALLENGING
TRANSITIONS AND
GAINING ADDITIONAL
PERSPECTIVE

I'm sure you have had an experience when a long-term coworker, or even maybe a friend, has left the company where you work. How was that departure carried out? Did the leadership team provide a clear and positive departure transition for that employee, or were there challenges experienced because of the employee's exit? Once that employee left the business, how was the team's morale influenced? Did the trust that the team had in the leadership group strengthen or weaken? There are scenarios when an employee's departure can have an impact on the remaining team based on how the leadership group manages the employee's exit from the business. In this chapter, I will share about a challenging exit that didn't need to occur, and the impact it had on the remaining team.

After my second near-death experience, I returned to work to another new structure within the organization. The leadership team I had worked closely with since my earlier return to the company had been dismantled, and an all-new team was in the process of being installed. The new team also determined that the structure we had in place would not fit what they wanted in their organization going forward, so everything I had been working with my director to build was being overhauled. It was time to take stock of my current situation and see if my long-term goals still aligned with the organization.

Realizing that what I had worked very hard over three years to help put in place for the future of the company was being systematically dismantled, I decided I wanted to close a skill gap I had in my résumé. While I had worked in the grocery store directly with customers, at a brokerage firm representing consumer packaged goods companies with retailers, and directly with consumer packaged goods manufacturers, I had never worked on the supplier side of market research providing insights to the manufacturers and retailers. Therefore, I started looking closely at the various vendors I'd worked with in my current role and narrowed down a list of potential employers to three. These three organizations were the top employers I felt could provide what I was looking for to close another knowledge gap.

Finalizing my list, I made the decision to pursue an organization where I had a passion for the work they did, I felt they were unique in the industry, and where there was still plenty of headroom to grow the business in the future. After meeting with the company's CEO, I joined the team as a vice president of research.

I was excited to jump in and learn a new side of the industry. What I did not anticipate was how much my new team would need to learn from me about how consumer packaged goods organizations worked within their insight teams. But this helped bring an element of fun to the new role! Being able to help others learn about the inner workings of consumer packaged goods, and helping set up those team members for success, was very rewarding for me. At the same time, I got to learn the processes of how to set up and activate learning plans for other organizations. While I had overseen research as a project manager for several years, I had not had the opportunity to function as a researcher in designing studies and implementing them within the marketplace.

Learning the nuances of how to do this effectively was both challenging and exciting.

Additionally, I was able to jump into a smaller start-up-style company and help put key people processes in place to ensure both strong team and individual development. I was able to lean on the processes I had found valuable over the years and help design a review format that would work for both entry-level and experienced individuals within the company. This helped set me up for a quick move into an SVP role.

What I did not anticipate with the move into the new organization were the challenges my old company would put me through. I had left the organization on good terms, or so I'd thought. I'd worked diligently up until my last day and had tried to make sure the team was set up for success, but I did not expect that my departure would be taken as personally as it was.

After I departed, I started receiving text messages and phone calls from former coworkers and friends telling me what had happened after I'd left. Once I was gone, the team had been informed that they were not permitted to talk to me or reach out to me for any reason. I still don't know what triggered this, but it was amusing and ironic that I found out because multiple people did exactly what they had been told not to do. They'd contacted me to make sure I was aware of what was happening.

This was a leadership lesson I learned by utilizing someone else's mistake. When one of your team members departs, be happy for them. Help them transition into their new role. While you may have challenges on your end because of their departure, treating them well helps showcase to your remaining team that you respect your team members and will support their decisions. Treating your departing team members poorly—directly to them or behind their back—only showcases to your remaining team members that you cannot be trusted. This could cause you additional departures or challenges with your leadership team if the attitude and team culture of your group deteriorates over time.

Within my new SVP role, I took on more responsibility for larger clients and for a larger team. While I still made mistakes that I learned from as a leader, we saw great success as a broader team and company within the marketplace. Additionally, I got the opportunity to speak at conferences across the country and met many new people within the industry. I had spent so many years focused on a couple of categories within the store, and the new "whole store" research opportunities provided me the chance to learn even more about shopper and consumer behaviors.

What's next? This is still to be determined, but I have learned valuable lessons from my latest post as well. Treat others how you want to be treated. Stand up for what is right, and don't blindly follow orders to make your life easier. Overcommunicate to your team about how they perform and how they are perceived in the company if you want them to succeed. Your team cannot improve in areas they are blind to or are unaware of. And finally, remember Ronald Reagan's words of wisdom from 1987, "Trust but verify."

FINAL THOUGHTS

While things in our lives don't always turn out as expected, there are lessons to be learned in every situation. When we go through challenges, we learn new things about ourselves and the world around us. Although some circumstances are harder than others, utilize those challenging moments as reflection points to determine what you have learned. All of us desire to be comfortable, but remember, there is no growth in comfort. Growth comes from the challenge!

I can recap my journey into four buckets of lessons learned:

1. Leading people
2. Effective communications and presentations
3. Career building
4. Life lessons

Leading People

Let's start with leading people. Leading others is a privilege, and something that takes an enormous amount of effort on the leader's part if they want to lead effectively. Learn as much as you can from others through classes, books, mentoring, etc. However, note that most of what will make you a good leader will come from doing. Being in the moment and learning from your team is an invaluable asset to sharpening your leadership skills. Also, don't wait until you are officially in a leadership position to behave like a leader. If you utilize the leadership skills you learn in your existing role before you're actually managing others, your promotion into that leadership role will happen more quickly.

Based on my on-the-job training, here are the lessons I have learned regarding leading people.

- Treat people with respect, talk to them the way you would want to be spoken to, and challenge others when they create hostile environments for you or your team. No one should ever feel like they are at risk of physical violence by a manager, and no one should be forced to endure verbal abuse.
- Realize that each person should only be held accountable for what is in their control.

- Always ask questions, and be open to hearing the answers.
    - As a leader, you must make sure you are open to hearing the full situation. You need to slow down and ensure you take in all the facts to make an informed decision. While there are times when a quick decision based on what you know is warranted, there are other more critical inflection points that require you to slow down. Don't hurt your company or your team members because you can't be bothered to take a moment and hear all the facts!
- Take the time to evaluate the leaders you've worked for, and create "emulate" and "avoid" lists of characteristics. Which column are you currently operating in?
- Ensure you understand what your team members are truly doing for your team, and publicly acknowledge their full contributions.
- Own your mistakes, and don't be afraid to say "I don't know" while you learn alongside your team.
- Stand up for what is right, and don't blindly follow orders to make your life easier.

- Overcommunicate to your team about how they perform and how they are perceived in the company if you want them to succeed. Your team cannot improve in areas they are blind to or unaware of, and you may be forced to oversee their departure.

- When one of your team members departs, be happy for them. Help them transition into their new role. While you may have challenges on your end because of their departure, treating them well helps showcase to your remaining team that you respect your team members and will support their decisions.

  - Treating your departing team members poorly—directly to them or behind their back—only showcases to your remaining team members that you cannot be trusted. This could cause you additional departures or challenges with your leadership team if the attitude and team culture of your group deteriorates.

Effective Communications and Presentations

Now, let's think about effective communications and presentations. Communicating effectively and being good at presenting are more challenging than most people realize. While many people feel they are good at giving presentations and keeping an audience's attention, I have found that most people are not. This can be a challenge for them to hear and an even bigger challenge for them to address. The challenge to address the issue is not because it is hard; it's because most people overcomplicate it or allow their nerves to get in the way.

There are many courses you can take and groups you can join to help sharpen your speaking skills, but here are the things I have learned and mentor others to utilize to be more effective.

- Put together your speaking points, back them up with facts and details, and provide your audience with a compelling argument. Utilize storytelling tactics to ensure your key points are remembered.
- Include emotional context and vocal inflections where relevant to provide a connection to your viewpoint.
- There is power in the pause. Take a breath. Allow information to sink in for your audience while you give yourself a moment to regroup in your head.
- Visuals are better than telling.
    - If able, get your audience in the moment with visuals (i.e., videos, images)

to showcase the key challenge. Let them see or hear it for themselves. It is hard to argue with what is right in front of them.

- Go to a local government meeting. This could be a zoning meeting, a school board meeting, or a council meeting in your area. See how the board members or local politicians' presentations or communication skills make you feel as an audience member.
  - What do you like?
  - What do you dislike?
  - How do they utilize facial expressions and tone? Is it effective in helping, or hurting, their communication?
  - Would you be moved to act on their recommendation or viewpoint? Why, or why not?

Going to a local government meeting, or getting involved directly, is a great way to learn about effective communication skills. Best of all, it is free.

Career Building
Third, let's discuss career building. Building your career is a challenging task. While some components are beyond your control, like layoffs or market conditions, there are things you can do even in those

circumstances to keep your career growing and on track.

Based on my experiences, here are some lessons you can consider when working on your own career development journey.

- Don't let others' opinions of you keep you from pursuing a dream! You can do anything you put your mind to if you are willing to work to get it. There will always be people who will judge a book by its cover rather than taking the time to understand the real person, but those people aren't worth your time or talent.

- Networking with others is incredibly valuable! Most of my career changes and growth came from jobs I never applied for; rather, they were from existing contacts who knew me and the work I could do for them. These contacts reached out to me to take roles that ended up challenging me and growing my skill set.

- Approach each meeting, internal or external, with a specific goal in mind. Whether building trust as a fact-based resource or going into a meeting with the goal of intentionally vocalizing input, utilize each meeting as an opportunity for growth. Your opportunities are influenced by others' observations of you! Use each moment to gain new advocates.

- As you progress through your career, find opportunities to cross-train into other functions when those moments become available. This can help you have additional experience and skill sets to more effectively navigate corporate restructuring. While a single experience-focused progression can allow you to build depth, it can leave you with few options should the organization deprioritize the function within the business.

- It's OK to "hold" at a company rather than making an immediate departure when things aren't going well or when reporting structures have changed. These moments can allow you to see structure opportunities and how you would do things differently. This can also allow you to potentially learn some key lessons: how not to lead an office or customer relationship, or how to work with others despite potentially awkward situations.

- Executive coaching can help showcase areas of growth you may not be aware of or may not have been coached on previously. If affordable, gaining insights from an impartial party on how you are perceived in your organization and how you can improve can be extremely helpful. Alternatively, getting 360-degree feedback can also provide insight into how you are perceived by others in your organization. Make sure to balance your 360-degree feedback across multiple levels including leadership above you, counterparts at your level, and your team members who report to you. Finally, ensuring feedback is 100 percent anonymous is important so your participants can be more focused on being open and honest with their input.

Life Lessons

Finally, let's look at the life lessons I've learned throughout my journey. Life lessons come in many different forms over time. They can be obtained through a challenging workplace, loss of loved ones, achieving seemingly impossible tasks, or even near-death experiences. However, life lessons can also come in those small, day-to-day events that you don't think much about when you're going through them but rather when you look back to reflect on past events. Therefore, take some time each year to reflect on past events and align them with where you are today. Was there a decision you made many years ago that seemed small at the time but ended up shaping several years of your life? Make sure to evaluate those moments and use them to help guide you in the future.

Some of the lessons in my life include the following.

- I have learned over the years that each of us has those times when something feels off. We have those moments when we have no real explanation for the steps we are about to take, but they just feel right. Trust those moments! They could literally change the course of your life!

- Understand when God is leading, and be willing to step out on faith to undertake the challenges He lays out for you. Be sensitive to His pull, and be open to doing what is required of you to make it happen. It will be worth it!

- Learning you can make it somewhere on your own without a family safety net can be very valuable to you. Having your family around is incredible and something to cherish, but knowing you can do it on your own if needed is powerful and liberating.

- Set clear goals, and make plans. I have found that when I don't have clarity about what I'm working toward, I find myself just existing. Take the time for goal setting and vision planning so you know what you are working toward.

- Wherever you go, understand local practices and expectations through observation and understanding, and act like a local. If you don't, be prepared to wait or take a back seat to someone else. No one is going to step in and help you. Help yourself!

- You can do whatever you want to do if you are focused, and you really work at it. All it takes is determination, preparation, and a willingness to be open to new things.

- Shifting your priorities in your career for family is OK and shouldn't be considered a detriment or hindrance. If the need arises for you to shift focus and prioritize your family, do it. You will be glad you did!

I hope you found something useful during our time together, and I wish you much success and happiness!

ABOUT THE AUTHOR

Nathaniel Noertker is a senior vice president of client consulting and services at Nailbiter Inc., an innovative leader in global market research. In his book, *Life and Leadership Lessons: From Rural America to Corporate Executive*, he shares his experiences and the valuable lessons he has learned throughout his journey, providing readers with his unique perspectives on leadership and personal growth.

With over thirty years of industry experience and over two decades in leadership roles, Nathaniel has held key positions in retailers' corporate headquarters, brokerage firms, consumer packaged goods manufacturers' offices for some of the world's top brands, and market research firms. His diverse background has equipped him with a comprehensive understanding of the industry's complexities and a keen ability to navigate its ever-changing landscape. It has also helped Nathaniel cultivate a holistic approach to success in today's competitive business environment.

Nathaniel is married, with two adult children and one grandson, and his roots in rural America continue to shape his values and outlook on life. Follow him at https://www.linkedin.com/in/nnoertker/.

www.ingramcontent.com/pod-product-compliance
Lightning Source LLC
Chambersburg PA
CBHW031521120626
46545CB00005B/1944